WADSWORTH PHILOSOPHERS SERIES

ON

EMERSON

David Justin Hodge
Harvard University

THOMSON
—✳—™
WADSWORTH

Australia • Canada • Mexico • Singapore • Spain • United Kingdom • United States

For more information about our
products, contact us at:
**Thomson Learning Academic
Resource Center
1-800-423-0563**

For permission to use material from
this text, contact us by:
**Phone: 1-800-730-2214
Fax: 1-800-731-2215
Web: www.thomsonrights.com**

Asia
Thomson Learning
5 Shenton Way #01-01
UIC Building
Singapore 068808

Australia
Nelson Thomson Learning
102 Dodds Street
South Street
South Melbourne, Victoria 3205
Australia

Canada
Nelson Thomson Learning
1120 Birchmount Road
Toronto, Ontario M1K 5G4
Canada

Europe/Middle East/South Africa
Thomson Learning
High Holborn House
50-51 Bedford Row
London WC1R 4LR
United Kingdom

Latin America
Thomson Learning
Seneca, 53
Colonia Polanco
11560 Mexico D.F.
Mexico

Spain
Paraninfo Thomson Learning
Calle/Magallanes, 25
28015 Madrid, Spain

On Emerson

(The Face of the) Preface

Introduction: On Finding One's Way About

(The Face of the) Preface

This book begins with an astonishing and appropriate equivocation, and it is the founding substance of nearly all works framed as "introductions to" a philosopher, namely, to see a person's name as representing a philosophy or line of thought. In Ralph Waldo Emerson, this equivocation becomes a celebrated and essential *equivalency*. To ask about the man is to come upon his manner. To inquire after the matter of his thinking is to encounter the matter of his being.

An introduction to Emerson thus should read like an intellectual or philosophical biography (even as Emerson's writing should read like philosophical *auto*biography). A text he produced ought to be situated in the context of its emergence. A problem ought to be grounded by a relation to the scene of its encounter. The benefit of this methodological approach is already evidenced in the title of the book, and in our habits of referring to philosophies with surnames. This arises when we shift between seeing "Emerson" as a name for a person who lived in the nineteenth century, and "Emerson" as shorthand for all the writing that that nineteenth century man wrote. To work through a thinker is to work through thoughts. And since those thoughts are not divorced from a body, it is also to work through the character of *that* text. The mobility of the human body is its own text, and issues the reader of discursive and polemical texts a chance to apprehend the import of this kind of performance.

The strategy here employed is one of integration and fusion. The vibrancy of written texts is folded together with the pulse of a once living man. What follows is not a recitation of quotations, but an implantation of words into the situations of engaged bodies. The purpose of these remarks is neither to paraphrase more lengthy biographies, nor to water down sophisticated philosophical criticism; rather, it is distill, in balanced measure, a multidimensional sense of Emerson—as writer and as a person. Such a distillation should instill a portrait composed of this man's life, his writings, and the times in which he lived. More as a consolation than a caution, therefore, do I say that the Emerson here conceived is both being and book. The surest way to make one's acquaintance with him is to consider the autobiographical nature of philosophical expression. The notion of "introducing" a figure is at once rendered more personal and intimate. I am not positioned as a mediating point between you, the reader, and Emerson, but a willing conversant in a mutual encounter. The same book of Emerson's writing that sits before me, sits there beside you. There is no privilege. In this respect, these introductory remarks are not rudimentary explanations of a complex system of thought, but a genuine invitation to engage with another person. In the context of this volume, let us call him Emerson.

D.J.H.

Cambridge, Massachusetts
December 31, 2001

Abbreviations of Emerson's Work
Cited Frequently

CP	*Collected Poems and Translations*
CS	*The Complete Sermons of Ralph Waldo Emerson*
CW	*The Complete Works of Ralph Waldo Emerson*
EA	*Emerson's Antislavery Writings*
EC	*The Correspondence of Emerson and Carlyle*
EJ	*Emerson in His Journals*
EL	*Essays and Lectures*
EP	*Emerson's Prose and Poetry*
J	*The Journals of Ralph Waldo Emerson*
L	*The Letters of Ralph Waldo Emerson*
SW	*The Selected Writings of Ralph Waldo Emerson*

INTRODUCTION: *On Finding One's Way About*

Orientation in unfamiliar places often requires more than one map. It can become apparent quickly that the angle of approach, and the course marked out will define one's relation to the site. And not always clearly or memorably. The interpretation of a text, or a life, can feel very much like reading a map: it aims to guide the reader through difficult terrain. But navigation is hampered, comprehension compromised, when the map and the place mapped appear different. The map is perhaps too detailed, or inversely, it may bear insufficient direction.

The disconnect in this analogy is, of course, that there are no fixed destinations in textual interpretation. Interpretation does not come to an end, for it seems no limits are found in navigating the topography of texts. One just keeps reading and reading, and with that attention, the text expands and deepens. The aim of an *introduction* to a text, to a person, therefore, should acknowledge that it is a preliminary map. Used rightly, it will serve as a guide to seek out other maps, and perhaps to write one's own.

One strategy for writing an introduction is to attend to a narrow segment of texts, going over them line by line, as if to tutor the reader in as many turns of phrase and allusions as possible. Another approach is to survey a wide span of texts, just briefly touching on them, as if to give the reader a glance. I work to avoid both methods—the first because it can go too deeply into textual analysis, alienating the reader through overdrawn detail; and, the second because it can scan the scene so quickly that the reader only gleans a superficial sense of what the work or the person is about. In this introduction, I attempt to write *between* these extremes. The result, it is intended, will be a series of remarks that cover a diverse range of topics and problems, texts and persons, times and spaces and yet, on occasion, plunge to mine a crucial point. I dwell, therefore, where it seems of service, and I move on more swiftly when remaining would mean—in the context of an introduction—either belaboring a claim, or indulging a tangent.

This introduction should serve several practical purposes in mapping the reader's relation to Emerson's life and work. It should provide some sense of his chronology, biography, prominent prose and poetry, friends and family, travels, social projects, private practices, cultural context, and central and abiding themes and thoughts. In the penultimate chapter, there is a collection of brief critical remarks by eminent literary and philosophical critics. And, perhaps most important to aid one's search for additional maps of Emerson's work—a bibliography selectively assembled to disclose a multiplicity of additional sites awaiting exploration and reading.

1

Boston, Harvard, and the Reluctant Reverend

In 1803, when Ralph Waldo Emerson was born at No. 27 Summer Street in Boston, there were about thirty thousand residents of the city. The Declaration of Independence was ratified only sixteen years earlier. Thomas Jefferson and John Adams were still alive and corresponding. Immanuel Kant was in Königsberg. And Beethoven finished "Kreutzer" (Opus 47), a sonata for violin and piano. In 1882, when Emerson died, at his home in Concord, Massachusetts, Franklin D. Roosevelt was born, Friedrich Nietzsche published *The Gay Science*, and Thomas Edison designed the first hydroelectric plant. By this time, the United States had survived a Civil War, and was on the threshold of applying a new range of technological instruments that would transform daily life—from electricity to radio, from the automobile to the telegraph, from the airplane to the moving image. Cross-Atlantic air travel would soon become commonplace, and the atom would be split a few decades later. A man would walk on the moon within ninety years. Alive in all but one of the decades of the nineteenth century, Emerson was as much alive to witness the changes in religion, science, politics, and letters as he was a conscientious catalyst by and through which Americans framed their relationship to themselves, and their developing roles.

This is all to say that Emerson, like Henry Adams, was born within reach of what seems antique life, and died at the very threshold of a new world. His distance from us in time makes him seem old fashioned, but, in context, his contact and comment upon the times shows him a distinctively modern thinker. In many cases, especially

1

those having to do with American identity and social transformation, he witnessed or wrote about what have come to be the defining crises and triumphs that have shaped the current era—the so-called postmodern. Emerson's engagement with his time, availed to us in his many essays, lectures, poems, letters, and journals, provides both a documentation and a critical comment upon the world with which he grew intimate. It is this rare combination of engagement and production that make Emerson of special relevance.

The events that compose Emerson's biography could hardly have been more dramatically scripted by Thomas Hardy or Henry James. And since, Emerson's writing is so intimately tied, indeed born out of, his contact with immanent life, it seems the surest and most satisfying way to approach his work is by attending to a narrative structure—a structure almost intrinsic to his development and scores of personal diaries. If Emerson's life makes a compelling story, then his writing makes a compelling series of remarks within that story—both of which are, somehow, made more interesting and intelligible when treated together, and in rough sequence.

But the synchronicity of Emerson's life and the span in which he lived it bears most heavily on the unique perspective these years afforded him. Granted, he could have neglected or been ill prepared to receive what occurred before him. It is thus the particular confluence of Emerson's impressions of that duration that help to make clearer just how profound a transition point it was that he stood upon. Indeed, we might regard Emerson as having occupied a peculiar shift in human history. This transition, at least in the United States, could be defined in several ways, say, from the agrarian to the metropolitan, or from the communal to the individual. But, for Emerson, there was a more distinctive character to the shift he engaged, namely, how theological worldviews were being overcome by technological and scientific ones.

From his earliest years, when he was struggling with the philosophy of David Hume, and later with the claims of Charles Lyell, Emerson endeavored to assimilate the controversies raised by skepticism and evolutionary theory into a thoroughgoing network of remarks on man, nature, and the influence of culture. His efforts were geared not merely to forge a system of reply, but to substantiate the idea that we ought not tip headlong towards science after having bent for so long in the opposite extreme. We ought, that is to say, not become skeptics in place of being dogmatists.

Emerson was raised in the expectation that he would succeed his father and grandfather in being a prominent Protestant minister in his home city of Boston. And for many years, the trajectory of his scholarship and personal intentions, would make it seem that he would fulfill that expectation, and perhaps exceed it. But like a sixteenth century astronomer who read Copernicus, or an early twentieth century physicist reading Einstein's paper on Brownian motion, Emerson had much to reckon with in the new science and philosophy of his day. Many of his class, but not his caliber, were content to dismiss the hurly-burly contestations that bit at their feet. Emerson was, contrariwise, disturbed. And the restlessness that swelled from that disturbance fueled his zeal to find effective and sustainable ways of mounting a response.

At first glance, the rigor and apparent neutrality of scientific method made religion seem irredeemably compromised by histories of personal preference and by superstitious habits. Religion was not a threat to scientific theory because science changed the criteria of belief to such an extent that religious faith was emptied of power, and drained of significance. By contrast, religion saw science, on most accounts, as at odds with faith, since it sought to adopt an attitude of constant revision and change. The unity of religious faith is possible only when a creed can be adopted, and faith in it can be assured. Apart from this, religion would seem altogether casual, lacking the sanctity that gives a belief its power.

An early trend of Emerson's thought is trying to negotiate a way in which the emotive insight of religious faith can be made sanguineous with the rational assertions of scientific theory. The process of creating an intermediary position would, however, change both positions, stripping religion of its conventions and science of its antisepticity. In trying to situate the new materialism and naturalism posed by science, with the seemingly irrelevant, dogmatism and superstition of spiritual life, Emerson forged a kind of rational spiritualism. It would work to recover and realign familiar elements of religion and science in such a way that they would no longer seem incompatible, but essentially interdependent. Emerson wished to be both a "poet" and a "naturalist," and thus to express the scientific miracle of nature through emotional insight. He made the object of his writing a fusion of apparent contraries: rational faith, and faith in reason. The defining reference for this coincidence was not God or scientific experiment, but experience in and through Nature. In his first book, *Nature*, he pulled seemingly incongruent cords together: "In the woods, we return to reason and faith" (*CW*, vol. I, 10). One's relation to oneself, others, religion, and science came to fruition only by way of one's core engagement with the natural world.

A portion of a poem from 1847 distills a thousand pages of essays and journal entries, to render an impression of what is wrong with a world split between faith and reason, religion and science. And why it is only through a personal perception of divinity in everyday experience, and a genuine inhabitation of immanent life, that the errors of the conflict are evaporated.

> O, that were much, and I could be a part
> Of the round day, related to the sun
> And planted world, and full executor
> Of their imperfect functions.
> But these young scholars, who invade our hills,
> Bold as the engineer who fells the wood,
> And traveling often in the cut he makes,
> Love not the flower they pluck, and know it not,
> And all their botany is Latin names,
> The old men studied magic in the flowers,
> And human fortunes in astronomy,
> And an omnipotence in chemistry,
> Preferring things to names, for these were men,
> Were unitarians of the united world
> And, wheresoever their clear eye-beams fell,
> They caught the footsteps of the SAME. Our eyes
> Are armed, but we are strangers to the stars.
> And strangers to the mystic beast and bird,
> And strangers to the plane and to the mine (*CP*, 111-2).

Emerson presides over this current condition of man, one that finds him equipped with "sick eyes." It is the fault of perception that leaves us unable to fathom the multidimensionality of nature, and of ourselves. The question for Emerson, and for his readers, is whether this writing becomes an encomium for a nature forever lost, and so a lament suffused with impotent nostalgia; or, whether this writing becomes a stirrup to the ribs of humanity, provoking us to reconsider our inheritances, and question radically whether we should *revise* our manner of inhabiting the world, which is to say—see it anew.

The Disunity of Unitarians

The liberal Protestants in Boston, known as Unitarians, are different from those "unitarians of the united world" to which Emerson refers in his poem, "Blight." The unitarians of the poem were those who could live unity in their lives and thinking. This is why they could

4

see the commonality of being in nature. The Unitarians, on the other hand, are perhaps unfortunately named, as the faith followed in their churches was, as in so many Protestant churches of the day, accosted by fragmentation of belief and by conflicting interpretations of what constituted not just religious faith, but Christian faith. If the Unitarians were united, if their faith was *a* faith, and their creed was singular, it would not have tolerated the shards of descent that factionalized it, especially in the years of Emerson's late adolescence when he was sensitive to the influence of his inherited faith, and its leading practitioners.

There were several distinctive Unitarian voices, which despite claiming loyalty to a common group name, reinforced strong lines of individual difference. Among the throng were three ministers who, in time, came to define the views that make clear the conflict over Unitarian faith.

William Ellery Channing [1780-1842] was Boston's most famous and influential Unitarian minister of his time, and preached at the Federal Street Church. Channing was an eloquent preacher, and a deft moral reasoner. His liberal viewpoints were just shy of radical, but sufficient to stoke the restless imaginations of his young audiences. Emerson was especially impressed by Channing's sermon "Unitarian Christianity" (1819), and "Likeness to God" (1829). In these and other works, Emerson admired Channing's challenge to the Christian faith, namely, asking the faithful to consider that humans are possessed of a rational nature that is capable of interpreting Scripture. The human mind, Channing argued, is not fated by God's decisions (as the Calvinist tradition held), but rather is equipped with a moral conscience sufficient to the task of forming and reforming human action. To ears sensitive to the implications of Channing's claims, his remarks were sufficiently radical to inspire the admiration of those who wished to reform their practices of faith, and the character of the Church.

Andrews Norton [1786-1853], Dexter Professor of Sacred Literature at Harvard Divinity School was, along with Channing, responsible for the curriculum at the Divinity School during the years Emerson attended. But that shared responsibility did not mean a shared outlook. Norton's massive work, *Evidences of the Genuineness of the Gospels*, attests to his concern that the liberal interpretation of the New Testament (of, for example, the validity of miracles, revelation, and the divinity of the narratives) undermined the foundation of Unitarian theology. Norton's orthodoxy contrasted sharply with Channing's views, and so, later, when Emerson began to voice his own critical remarks on Christianity, and Unitarian Christianity in particular,

Norton spoke of him with unapologetic reprimand. He decried Emerson's *Address* at Harvard Divinity School as symptomatic of the corrosive forces at work among the liberal, radical Unitarians. Norton countered that such remarks merely contributed to the "latest form of infidelity" (Howe, 90). In the early 1830's, one of Emerson's friends and classmates, George Ripley [1802-1880], engaged Norton in a debate about revised notions of revelation and miracles. For his position, Norton considered Ripley an infidel. Some years later, in 1840, Ripley wrote *Letters on the Latest Form of Infidelity*, in which he replied to Norton's reproval of Emerson.

Henry Ware, Jr. [1794-1843] was preaching at the Second Church in Boston when, in 1829, he was invited to assume the Professorship of Pulpit Eloquence and Pastoral Care at Harvard Divinity School. Eager to accept this position, he resigned from the Second Church, and helped funnel Emerson into his former post. Several years later, however, in the aftermath of Emerson's delivery of the *Address* to the Divinity School (1837), the conservative Ware joined Norton in castigating Emerson for his views, deeming them at once dismissive of Scripture and overly literary. Ware's best-known work, *The Formation of the Christian Character* (1831), outlines his idea of Unitarian religiosity, saying, in part, that Jesus is the proper model of human conduct, and that we should aim to imitate him to the greatest degree possible. Ware argues that the surest way to reinforce the religious principles derived from such imitation is to develop habits that will reinforce them.

In Channing, Norton, and Ware, we can see the contemporary local views that infiltrated Emerson's immediate life, whether at church, at school, or in the company of peers. Alongside a still prominent, though waning, mood of Calvinist doctrine—often strained through complex histories of founding Puritan figures and traditions—Emerson's thinking about theology and ethics, philosophy and aesthetics was largely bathed in the turbulent and debris-filled waters that ran through Boston and Cambridge, and therefore through the locks of early nineteenth century American spirituality and religious experience.

Journey through Harvard, Journal at Harvard

Emerson's formal education shows that his intellectual interests and passions accorded with the standard curriculum of young Harvard men. And yet, he also reached beyond this to a steadfast ecumenism. His readings were disparate. And his writings became, even in his late teens, a remarkable stage of combination and comparison. Seemingly fueled by a strident concern about value theory—both in ethical and

6

aesthetic terms—Emerson wrote as if to mine the great texts of the past for their possible contribution to present crises on the same or similar issues. He read widely in Plato [c.428-347 BCE], Plutarch [ACE 46?-120?], the Stoics—especially Marcus Aurelius [ACE 121-80] and Seneca [c.2 BCE-ACE 65], Michel de Montaigne [1533-92], John Locke [1632-1704], David Hume [1711-1776], Johann Wolfgang von Goethe [1749-1832], William Wordsworth [1770-1850], and Samuel Taylor Coleridge [1772-1834]. The outlines of German Romanticism were filtered through to him from his professors Edward Everett and George Ticknor. And Emerson was introduced to Scottish Common Sense philosophy—Thomas Reid [1710-9] and Richard Price [1723-91]—by his philosophy professors, Levi Frisbie and Levi Hedge (McLeer, 55). In his extracurricular time, Emerson read in Shakespeare [1564-1616] and Byron [1788-1824].

While living on Harvard Yard, residing in Hollis Hall (adjacent to Harvard Hall and Holden Chapel), and despite a well-known pedigree, Emerson was comparatively poor. He worked as an assistant to the President of the College in trade for his room. President Kirkland, a classmate or Emerson's father, had Emerson live at his home during freshman year, and made sure the young Emerson had work and adequate funding. In his senior year, Emerson remained in Hollis Hall to live with his freshman brother, Edward [1805-1834], while his classmates moved to Holworthy Hall. His older brother, William [1801-1868] ran a small grammar school in Boston for girls where Emerson would frequently work in an adjunct capacity. After the death of his father William [1769-1811], Emerson's mother, Ruth Haskins Emerson [1768-1853] was left without a source of income, and so relied on boarders to maintain the household and to send all her children, except the mentally incapacitated Bulkeley [1807-1859], to Harvard College. Despite the admirable fortitude of Emerson's mother, she still relied on wage contributions from her abler sons. And Emerson, like all his brothers, dutifully helped maintain Ruth and her household, even after they left her care.

In his late teen years, while studying, working at the College, and helping at home, Emerson began to keep a journal. This common practice might be unworthy of remark save the fact that Emerson invested so much of himself in this habit. Not only would his journal, which he initially titled "Wide World," become a repository for his own thoughts, it would also serve as a catch-all for remarks by others, quotations from letters and books, and the fertile platform upon which he began experimenting with poetic expression. Ambitious in scope and content from its commencement, Emerson kept to his journals with continual addition for the next fifty years of his life. As he matured, and as his writing prospects and projects changed, Emerson did not abandon this initially youthful exercise. Instead, he adjusted it to suit his current and evolving manner of composition. Importantly, his journals served as the default source from which he drew much of the material that would come to form his most significant contributions to American letters and ideas. Here, in his common practice of culling from his journals, a sentiment, and many of the words that carry it, makes its way from the private page to a published essay:

> A great genius must come & preach self reliance. Our people are timid, desponding, recreant whimperers. If they fail in their first enterprises they lose all heart. If the young merchant fails, men say he is RUINED. If the finest genius studies at the Cambridge Divinity College, and is not ordained within a year afterwards in Boston, or New York, it seems to his friends & himself that he justified in being disheartened & in complaining for the rest of his life (May 27, 1839; two days after Emerson's thirty-sixth birthday. *EJ*, 218).

And in "Self-Reliance," first published in 1841, he writes:

> If our young men miscarry in their first enterprises, they lose all heart. If the young merchant fails, men say he is *ruined*. If the finest genius studies at one of our colleges, and is not installed in an office within a year afterwards in the cities or suburbs of Boston or New York, it seems to his friends and to himself that he is right in being disheartened, and in complaining for the rest of his life (*EL*, 275).

But such direct coincidence of shared words is not the end of the transferal. There are numerous occasions when the private is converted into a form deemed appropriate for public display. Upon losing his first wife, Ellen, Emerson shifts the specifics of his emotional pain to a general comment on the pain of losing others in death, on the character of marriage, and the nature of mutual harmony through love. A few days after Ellen died, he wrote in his journal:

> O willingly, my wife, I would like down in your tomb. But I have no deserts like yours, no such purity, or singleness of heart. Pray for me Ellen & raise the friend you so truly loved, to be what you thought of him. When your friends or mine cross me, I

8

comfort myself by saying, you would not have done so. Dear
Ellen (for that is your name in heaven) shall we not be united even
now more & more, as I more steadfastly persist in the love of truth
& virtue which you loved? Spirits are not deceived & now you
know the sins & selfishness which the husband would fain have
concealed from the confiding wife—help me to be rid of them;
suggest good thoughts as you promised me, & show me truth. Not
for the world, would I have left you here alone; stay by me & lead
me upward. Reunite us, o thou Father of our Spirits (February 13,
1831; she died on the eighth. *EJ*, 74).

A decade later, in his essay, "Love," also from *Essays: First Series*
(1841), Emerson makes generic a swirl of imagery relating to his
defense against the threat of losing his love, his grief when such love is
lost, and his hope that such love may find another incarnation:

The lovers delight in endearments, in avowals of love, in
comparisons of their regards. When alone, they solace themselves
with the remembered image of the other. . . . They try and weigh
their affection, and, adding up costly advantages, friends,
opportunities, properties, exult in discovering that willingly,
joyfully, they would give all as a ransom for the beautiful, the
beloved head, not one hair of which shall be harmed. . . .
At last they discover that all which at first drew them
together,—those once sacred features, that magical play of
charms,—was deciduous, had a prospective end, like the
scaffolding by which the house was built; and the purification of
the intellect and the heart, from year to year, is the real marriage,
foreseen and prepared from the first, and wholly above their
consciousness (*EL*, 335-7).

This kind of undenied and explicit self-borrowing makes Emerson's
published writings possess an enviable personal resonance. Depending
on one's direction of reading—whether first in the journals, and then in
the lectures and essays; or, the other way around—the division between
private and the public, the personal and shared, is ambiguous; indeed,
such division is, one might say, actively, even daringly tempted to
dissolution. Emerson's published writings, at times, bear the weight of
confession. And yet, the anonymity afforded by concepts appears to
protect him again and again from reminding us of his particular
situation, and so—reminding us of our own. Reading the journals
alongside the essays, reinforces the amount of personal investment

9

Emerson makes in his work.   Still, in the writing submitted to others, the work that exceeds the boundaries of his tabletop or pocket journal, he coaxes from his individual experience comment and critique that insists its relevance to the lives of communities beyond his immanent domain and his own time.   In this respect, Emerson adapted, perhaps intuitively and not intentionally, the practice of such conversion that he read in Aurelius' *Meditations*, Augustine's *Confessions*, and Montaigne's *Essays*.

Teaching Lessons

In 1821, after college graduation, at age eighteen, Emerson joined his elder brother, William, at the school for girls he established in Boston.   For the next few years, Emerson taught.   But he also kept to his journals, and tried his hand at contributing to a leading Unitarian publication, *The Christian Disciple*.   But when William, enthusiastic to study theology, departed for Göttingen, Emerson was left to run the school by himself.   In William's absence, Emerson arrived at some rather dire self-estimations, perhaps fearing that teaching was not his calling, and that writing would not issue from him as he wished it to. Having lived a bit more than two decades, he writes with a dramatic intensity that would suggest he was sure he had seen his future:

> The dreams of my childhood are all fading away & giving place to some very sober & very disgusting views of a quiet mediocrity of talents & condition—nor does it appear to me that any application of which I am capable, any efforts, any sacrifices could at this moment restore any reasonableness to the familiar expectations of my earlier youth (September 1823. *EJ*, 36).

Teaching enabled Emerson to contribute more significantly to keeping his mother's household, and to aiding his younger brothers Edward Bliss and Charles Chauncy through their college years.   But the work tested Emerson's patience, and did not inspire him.   "I am a hopeless school-master . . . toiling through this miserable employment without even the poor satisfaction of discharging it well" (Cabot, vol. I, 72-3). William's departure for Europe only made the contrast between lives more emphatic, and, one could suspect, helped Emerson justify closing his brother's school in order to pursue further his own theological education.

Out of Sight at Harvard Divinity School

In 1825, a still young Emerson entered Harvard Divinity School, itself an institution formed only a few years earlier. He lived in Room #14 of the newly constructed Divinity Hall, lonely but dignified at the periphery of Harvard Yard. Upstairs, thirteen years later, in the hall's chapel, Emerson would deliver his *Address*. For the young Emerson, at twenty-two, delivering a soul-stirring, controversial speech to his fellow classmates and valued professors, was yet far away. In these days, the crisis at hand was more proximate, as he was scandalized by his own doubts in attending the school, and following after a career in the ministry. And also put upon by his frail health, and that of several in his family. Emerson was not on campus for long before his body interfered with his studies: attacked by uveitis (a swelling of the eye), Emerson temporarily went blind, and thus was unable to read, and therefore to study. He returned to teaching for the remainder of the year, and in early 1826 resumed his studies at the Divinity School. By October, he was approbated to preach, but delayed his turn at the pulpit as he was stricken by several severe conditions, including pleurisy (a lung ailment), rheumatism, and diarrhea. Each of these dire infringements upon his health appeared related to tuberculosis. By the spring of 1827, he was well enough to return to New England after a spell of convalescence in the South, and began preaching in Boston and in surrounding towns and suburbs. At the end of 1827, on one of his visits to Concord, New Hampshire, he met Ellen Louisa Tucker. A year later, they were engaged.

Post at the Pulpit

As the 1820's drew to a close, Emerson's prospects appeared to be improving. He seemed to have escaped the immediate peril of tuberculosis (even though suffering several of its related severe, but nonfatal effects), made his way through training in the ministry, and was on the verge of taking up one of Boston's most prominent and prized pastorships, that of Henry Ware, Jr. And he had fallen in love. For a two-year period, between early 1829 and early 1831, the same world that made him despair of his future now seemed primed to receive him. In this brief interval, he was married, assumed duties at the same church were Increase and Cotton Mather had preached, and began to give sermons in which he spoke if not with unqualified confidence, then at least with some impression that his situation was mending—perhaps even on the verge of flourishing. In his brief career

11

as a minister, Emerson wrote one hundred seventy-eight sermons. During the last few years of the 1820's and into the early 1830's, one can trace the arc of Emerson's engagement with the immanent Unitarian Christianity, and with the spiritual heritage of Puritan Calvinists. Emerson was intimately acquainted with both strains of New England religiosity, the former mainly through William Ellery Channing, and the latter, primarily through Emerson's aunt Mary Moody Emerson [1774-1863].

The conflict between orthodox Calvinists and liberal Unitarians was at a crescendo in the years in which Emerson was forming his own vision of religion. The controversy to be adjudicated was where humans stood in relation to themselves and to divinity. Emerson, like Channing and Ware, affirmed the Unitarian position, which sees character development, or "self-culture" (as Emerson would later call it in "Self-Reliance"), as the initial ground of religion. Personal salvation was not shuttled off to God's discretion, but was retrieved and framed as having to do with human will (not divine grace). In Sermon XIV (Emerson numbered, but did not title his sermons), from 1828, Emerson explicitly denies the Calvinist creed of human depravity, replacing it with a Unitarian view where Jesus is a moral exemplar—the premier referent for religious guidance, and therefore, human action.

First a denial of the Calvinist theology of depravity:

> We have not so learned the lessons of Christ as to think that the sin of Adam had poisoned the blood of all the race of man; had called down the wrath of the Almighty upon them all without reference to their character; had turned their good to evil, their prayers to blasphemies, their hope to horror (*CS*, 152).

Then, a revision of what is revealed in Scripture:

> We have learned that the scriptures teach none of these things, but that the purpose of the scripture is to reveal to us the will of God, to give us the cheering revelation that our souls are immortal; that this world is a state of discipline, a school of preparation to train us up for endless being; that all we do goes to make up our character, and that on our character, our happiness wholly depends (*Ibid.*).

And, lastly, an affirmation of the Unitarian appraisal of Jesus, and his relevance to human life:

12

For this, we believe, the Son of God came into the world—to teach us these truths, and to give us in *his* life, a model for ours (*CS*, 152).

In the first and second excerpts, we can hear echoes of William Ellery Channing's "Unitarian Christianity" and in the third, an anticipation of Henry Ware's *Formation of Christian Character*. The lesson of this sermon, like so many others that Emerson preached, is, therefore, fundamentally *ethical* in nature. Emerson's religious sentiments are formed under the bright lights of the Second Great Awakening—a movement in the first third of the nineteenth century that emphasized the *revealed* nature of God. But Emerson tempers this liberal turn by saying that such revelation comes to naught if we do not apply it to lived experience. In the same sermon, he cauterizes this point:

> But the main duty, my brethren, which arises out of the possession of religious knowledge (and all that makes the subject of any practical value) is to use that knowledge as the guide of our own conduct. Indeed, my friends, unless this is the end of inquiry all our zeal to find the truth and all our exaltation in the possession is solemn trifling. It is a small thing that we know; we must practice also (*CS*, 153).

The urgency of Emerson's liberal appeal would be extended and refined during the course of his pastorship, culminating, at last, in his views exceeding the limits of liberal Unitarianism. Emerson's formidable skill as a minister, and the approbation of his colleagues and parish, could not quell his internal conflicts—as related to securing a vocation as to finding a defensible use of his voice. This spiritual infraction was further complicated by his and his young wife's bodily traumas.

Though Emerson married Ellen, who in her late teens was several years younger than he, knowing that she had tuberculosis, there was an implied hope that her age and her willful intention could surmount any mortal threat. Though Emerson assumed a role as minister of Boston's Second Church afflicted by his own (suspected) tubercular conditions and by his ongoing doubts about his faith, there was an expectancy in his action that such scourges would pass. In time, it was presumed, Ellen's somatic disease would retreat as Emerson's spiritual illness would be rendered benign.

2

Love, Death, and the Germ of *Nature*

Emerson's turn of fortune was short-lived, and by early 1831 the life he and Ellen fought to insist upon retreated without apology or explanation. Despite a whispering doubt in his wife's health, and his faith as a minister, Emerson tried to live reticently, preparing, it seems, more for recovery than demolition. By the end of 1832, Emerson had no wife, no job, little money, and seemed bereft both of his love and his calling.

If his world collapsed, it is in this period that Emerson begins to remake it. In the years following Ellen's death, Emerson surveyed the ruins he inherited, including Ellen's corpse, Europe, and a spectrum of Western literature and philosophy. Out of these encounters, he fashioned a new life. In large measure, this reconstruction was managed by revision, that is, by seeing things in a new way. Such seeing is not just formative but reforming. Seeing constitutes being: "What we are, that only can we see" (*EL*, 48). In the last chapter of *Nature*, entitled "Prospects," we see Emerson looking ahead (not looking back). He has lost much, but realized that the state of his constitution is yet fortifiable.

> You also are a man. Man and woman, and their social life, poverty, labor, sleep, fear, fortune, are known to you. Learn that none of these things is superficial, but that each phenomenon has its roots in the faculties and affections of the mind. Whilst the abstract question occupies your intellect, nature brings it in the concrete to be solved by your hands. It were a wise inquiry for the

14

closet, to compare, point by point, especially at crises in life, our daily history, with the rise and progress of ideas in the mind (*EL*, 48).

It is thus a prospective and not a retrospective idea, a constructive and not a destructive idea, that restores Emerson: "Build, therefore, your own world" (*Ibid.*). A world, one might say, that can be built out of faith in oneself apart from a faith in others, traditions, past ages, and the haunting influence of so many ruins.

The End of Ellen and the Ecclesia

The optimism for recovery from serious illness, so precious to one's regard for the other, is hastily and harshly dismissed when death prevails. When, on February 8, 1831, Ellen drew her last blood-strewn breaths, and spoke with earnest support and mercy for her husband, the life they conceived for themselves was lost. Emerson wrote of her final words in his journal:

> Never had any one spake with greater simplicity or cheerfulness of dying. She said, 'I pray for sincerity & that I may not talk, but may realize what I say.' She did not think she had a wish to get well, & told me "she should do me more good by going than by staying; she should go first & explore the way, & comfort me" (February 13, 1831. *EJ*, 75).

The balance of the year was spent keeping to the outward form of his just accepted duties at the Second Church. But he was changed. Every morning, Emerson would walk to Ellen's tomb, as if to make an appointment he felt must be kept. Such a ritual of grieving left him time to walk and to think, and thus to contemplate how to continue in Ellen's absence. More than a year after Ellen died, on March 28, 1832, Emerson wrote one line in his journal:

> I visited Ellen's tomb & opened the coffin (*EJ*, 82).

In that day's entry, there are no further details about what he saw, nor any remarks about how he felt. Regardless, the encounter reinforced Emerson's questions concerning the finality of his separation from Ellen. If she were still alive, Emerson might yet have come to a similar concern about his place in the ministry. But her death hastened his confrontation with the church. The propriety of marriage

15

was gone, and the mourner's revaluation of things became increasingly apparent. By the summer of 1832, Emerson became more vocal about the status of his vocation. Privately, he worked through doubts concerning his adaptability to the job. Publicly, he began to question protocols of worship. Privately, he conceded his doubt:

> I have sometimes thought that in order to be a good minister it was necessary to leave the ministry. The profession is antiquated. In an altered age, we worship in the dead forms of our forefathers. Were not a Socratic paganism better than an effete superannuated Christianity? (June 2, 1832. *EJ*, 83).

Less than two years after taking over for Henry Ware, Jr. at the Second Church, Emerson stood precipitously on the edge of either being dismissed from the church, or dismissing himself from it. He wrote an essay entitled "The Lord's Supper" in which he questioned the relevance of the Eucharist to modern worship. Using Scripture as evidence, he sought to show that Jesus meant the Transubstantiation of bread (into body) and blood (into wine) to hold *only* for The Last Supper. Its significance, he argued, is tied to that occasion (not to its imitation generation after generation). Emerson weighted his explanation with evidence from Scripture that he believed stood in favor of his position; these remarks, mainly relating to inconsistencies in the transmission of ritual, find Emerson in his role as minister. In these cases, he is trying to defend his wish to abstain from the Communion by means that will be forthcoming to his audience and the clerics who oversee his work. And yet, by the end of the sermon, one hears his defense shift from ritual and Scripture to conscience.

> The statement of this objection leads me to say that I think this difficulty, wherever it is felt, to be entitled to the greatest weight. It is alone a sufficient objection to the ordinance. It is my own objection. This mode of commemorating Christ is not suitable to me. That is reason enough why I should abandon it (*SW*, 107).

After his painstaking criticism of Scripture, and the presentation of his reinterpretation of this ritual, Emerson announced that such justifications are *secondary* to his finding the custom unsuitable to him. Such an appeal suppresses the conventional power associated with reason (based on dogmatic texts and principles) and (external) authority. In this way, Emerson's appeal to an internal authority provides an important glimpse of ideas that will be developed en force in the next decade. Emerson continues:

> If I believed it was enjoined by Jesus on his disciples, and that he
> even contemplated making permanent this mode of
> commemoration, every way agreeable to an Eastern mind, and yet
> on trial it was disagreeable to my own feelings, I should not adopt
> it. I should choose other ways which, as more effectual upon me,
> he would approve more. For I choose that my remembrances of
> him should be pleasing, affecting, religious. I will love him as a
> glorious friend, after the free way of friendship, and not pay him a
> stiff sign of respect, as men do those whom they fear (*SW*, 107).

Even if Emerson's biblical hermeneutics is a failure, and even if the
inverse of his view is persuasively shown, the condition of his protest
will remain unaltered. Performing the Eucharist is "disagreeable" to
him because, he feels, it corrupts the kind of relationship he wishes to
have with Jesus: not one between mendicant and Lord, but one
between friends.

"The Lord's Supper" may be taken as the first public occasion of
Emerson's career in which he clearly inhabits the role of cultural critic,
and reformer of values. And it would have immediate and drastic
consequences. Prior to delivering this sermon, Emerson asked leaders
of the Unitarian Church if they would consider allowing him to abstain
from performing these rites. By the time he pronounced his views
publicly, it was made clear to him that they would not accept his
revision. With hesitation and regret, they denied his request. Soon
after, in October 1832, Emerson respectfully resigned from his pulpit,
and from the Unitarian Church. And in December of the same year,
just a few days before leaving for Europe, Emerson wrote a letter to his
church in which he expressed his endearing affection for them, and his
anguish that they could not continue as they had. Emerson took full
responsibility for his decision, laying no blame upon them, or the
Church. His letter, which he knew would reach a diverse audience,
accommodates their disappointment through apology. His endearments
are so clear and strong that it is difficult to see why he insists that he
must leave. Thus, what remains unsaid in this letter—for example,
concerning his doubts about his faith in the Church—is as significant as
what is said.

There is a moment in this last-minute letter when Emerson mounts
a fierce self-appraisal of his recent life. These confessional remarks,
more than any other in the letter, bear the weight of his emotional and
vocational crises. They admit his pitiful position, and elicit the

sympathy of those who may be compelled to denigrate him for his withdrawal. His hyperbole only serves to emphasize the tenderness of the time for him—both in his decision to leave the church, and in his decision to leave America.

> Our connexion has been very short. I had only begun my work. It is now brought to a sudden close, and I look back, I own, with a painful sense of weakness, to the little service I have been able to render, after so much expectation on my part,—to the chequered space of time, which domestic affliction and personal infirmities have made yet shorter and more unprofitable.
>
> As long as he remains in the same place, every man flatters himself, however keen may be his sense of his failures and unworthiness, that he shall yet accomplish much; that the future shall made [sic] for the past; that his very errors shall prove his instructors,—and what limit is there to hope? But a separation from our place, the close of a particular career of duty, shuts the books, bereaves us of this hope, and leaves us only to lament how little has been done (December 22, 1832. *L*, vol. VII, 211-2).

The outward circumstances of the controversy and the resignation give the impression that Emerson hinged his entire career (and indeed much of his formal education) on this one interpretive nuance (viz., the Lord's Supper). But inwardly, judged at least from his journals and letters, this conflict was symbolic. There were other problems, but this one was enough to illustrate his frustration with inherited dogmas and his resistance to the thinking that tends to prevail in groups. Emerson's resignation was not born from a hasty emotional reaction, even though it came to pass with haste.

In less than two years from the time he married Ellen, Emerson's former world seemed returned to him. He was alone. And he was in doubt. But it was a different world, since he had passed through the life-altering membranes of Ellen's death and his resignation from the church. He was marked by their lasting residues, but at the same time, and perhaps by their influences, able to take risks that no married Boston minister could justify.

Convalescence in Europe

In the late spring of 1831, Alexis de Tocqueville [1805-1859] arrived in the United States. Tocqueville had come on a mission to diagnose the state of things in America for his French contemporaries. His nine-month term abroad yielded *Democracy in America*. Emerson was on a similar trip, though heading the other way. Emerson's nine-month gestation proved comparably fecund. Through these bi-continental expeditions, the concept and actual life of America received some of its finest criticism. "The American Scholar" later appeared as the precipitate of Emerson's view of America from abroad.

On December 27, 1831, Charles Darwin [1809-1882] sailed out of England on the *Beagle*. Over the course of the next five years, he would gather a lifework's worth of data, and lay the ground from which he developed evolutionary theory. Two days shy of a year later, Emerson sailed away from his shores. He was not in search of theories, but experience. It turns out that, like Darwin, he encountered both. Emerson's aspiration to be a naturalist achieved its first significant incarnation in *Nature*.

On Christmas Day, 1832, Emerson boarded a ship bound for Europe. The decision to leave was conceived impetuously, and was made, understandably, to put some distance between him and the recent events. But the voyage itself was possessed of anything but alacrity. Buffeted about the ocean, pushed from side to side, slowed down and speeded up by wind currents, the brig Jasper made the Old World seem a planetary distance away. While a modern jet can shuttle one from Boston to Malta in twelve hours, it took Emerson nearly six weeks to do the same with his mode of conveyance. And if we may be bold enough to complain of stiff joints and poor food, consider Emerson's travel quarters: soiled by sea and shipman, fed from vats of salted foods, absent a bath and toilet, and cramped by a gathering of unknown seafarers. The trip, thus, did not only possess the metaphorical risks we find in retrospect, but also held literal risks. The captain was not exaggerating—or playing with tropes—when he spoke doubtfully of Emerson's making it to Europe alive (Richardson, 131). Emerson arrived in Malta on February 2, 1833. Several of his fellow passengers did not.

Once on land, after almost two additional weeks in ship-bound quarantine, Emerson began a tour of Sicily. After a month in Sicily, he boarded his first steam ship, which brought him from Messina to Naples, the city that he made his doorway to continental Europe. Working his way north, he accumulated sites that had until that time been present only to his imagination, and presented by ancient texts. He kept a textual companion on this trip, but it was not Livy or Horace, rather Goethe and his travel reminiscences, *Italian Journey*. Emerson passed through Herculaneum, Pompeii, then went further to Rome for a month where Boston's civil history was dwarfed by a colossus that spanned millennia. Then to Florence for a month. He was in Bologna in late May, and afterwards went to Ferrara. Before arriving in Venice on the first of June, he visited Petrarch's house in the Eugenean Hills near Padua. In Venice he confided to his journal "I am speedily satisfied with Venice. It is a great oddity—a city for beavers—but to my thought a most disagreeable residence" (June 1, 1833. *J*, vol. IV, 186). The Italian leg of his journey ended in Milan, by way of Verona and Brescia. He turned into Switzerland, stopping in Geneva, before spending a month in Paris. He ended his tour with a month and a half in England. But in Rome . . .

He roamed the streets and navigated the halls, as if life itself were made a museum. The city seemed an old friend introduced by other means—not by Latin schoolbooks, but by statuary and churches, paintings and temples. In his pocket journal, Emerson wrote:

> Rome fashions my dreams. All night I wander amidst statues & fountains, and last night was introduced to Lord Byron! It is a graceful termination to so much glory that Rome now in her fallen state should be the metropolis of the arts. Art is here a greatest interest than any where else. The Caffés are filled with English, French, & German artists, both sculptors & painters (April 13, 1833. *J*, vol. IV, 159).

And yet, while Emerson was overwhelmed with his encounters, either in waking life or in dreams, he was also registering disappointments. Lost illusions were translated into critical comments on culture. After attending a ceremony at The Sistine Chapel, with an apparently semi-lucid Pope presiding over the service, Emerson noted:

> It was hard to recognize in this ceremony the gentle Son of Man who sat upon an ass amidst the rejoicings of his fickle countrymen.

And then, widening his critique, he continues:

> All this pomp is conventional. It is imposing to those who know the customs of courts & of what wealth & of what rank these particular forms are the symbols. But to the eye of an Indian I am afraid it would be ridiculous. There is no true majesty in all this millinery & imbecility. Why not devise ceremonies that shall be in as good & manly taste as their churches & pictures & music? (March 31, 1833. *J*, vol. IV, 153).

As a tourist familiar with New England's Protestant churches—with their white walls and clear windows—the Roman Catholic *duomos* were perceivably both impressive and garish. Still, Emerson saw the artistry of the edifices as overcoming the impositions of religion (as if the inherited and anticipated religious content of a painting by Michel Angelo, for example, could not interfere with his creative skill and refined execution). But in witness to the workings of the papacy, and those who supported it, Emerson was less able to justify what he saw: the ritual overwhelmed the ritualizers. He discovered how foreign he was. He, at last, saw that there could be a breach between the ancient world and his familiar commonwealth. History would maintain a continuity, but for Emerson these sights proved alien and unattractive.

Even with his misgivings about the dominance of and distortion by the traditions that ruled Italy, just after leaving, he indulged in some rueful nostalgia, already having arrived in Paris:

> . . . I was sorry to find that in leaving Italy I had left forever that air of antiquity & history which her towns possess & in coming hither had come to a loud modern New York of a place (June 20, 1833. *J*, vol. IV, 197).

As early as 1833, we can already begin to hear the clang and spark of industrialization coming into aural prominence. Dense concentrations of people, buildings going higher, and the chatter of machinery begin to surround the urban dweller, and become—as here noted—even more distinctive for the traveler who arrives from the tranquil Italian countryside, or from the even less disturbed farmlands of Massachusetts Bay.

It may then not surprise that Emerson found great solace, and a fair measure of inspiration, in one of Paris' refuges from the bustling metropolis: The Garden of Plants. He was justifiably mesmerized by the Cabinet of Natural History, which was both comprehensive and well mounted. It seemed the very juxtaposition of so many diverse creatures made a statement about the peculiarity of life, human or otherwise.

> The limits of the possible are enlarged, & the real is stranger than the imaginary. . . . Here we are impressed with the inexhaustible riches of nature. The universe is a more amazing puzzle than ever as you glance along the bewildering series of animated forms,—the hazy butterflies, the carved shells, the birds, beasts, fishes, insects, snakes,—& the upheaving principle of life everywhere incipient in

the very rock aping organized forms. Not a form so grotesque, so savage, nor so beautiful but is an expression of some property inherent in man the observer,—an occult relation between the very scorpions and man. I feel the centipede in me—cayman, carp, eagle, & fox. I am moved by strange sympathies, I say continually "I will be a naturalist" (July 13, 1833. *J*, vol. IV, 200).

By November, later in the same year, Emerson was back in Boston giving a lecture on "The Uses of Natural History." As Charles Lyell's [1795-1897] geological theories were coming to bear (antagonistically) on creationist accounts of the earth's age, and Charles Darwin was sailing toward his introduction to the Galapagos' finches and, thereafter, moving nearer to his epoch-shaping theory of evolution, Emerson was making a very different use of natural history. While Lyell and Darwin sought to expose nature's underlying methods and order (if also admitting that such order is predicated on randomness and arbitrariness), Emerson worked to show man's necessary connection to that system. In this way, Emerson's efforts, seen first in his first book *Nature*, but also as late as his last (posthumous) book *Natural History of Intellect* (the name drawn from a series of lectures he delivered at Harvard in 1870), are much closer in spirit to the thought of ancient Stoics than to his contemporaries in the natural sciences. Nature's most salient service to man is in making evident his limitations. The "limits of the possible are enlarged;" they are not infinite. In concert with the sentiments of Seneca, Epictetus [55?-135?], and Marcus Aurelius, Emerson drew physics and logic into accord with ethics. The ancient use of physics and logic—here referred to as "natural history"—is reinscribed to show the inherent communion between human beings and the environment in which they persist, and potentially, thrive.

Emerson's reorientation in Europe continued when he visited England and Scotland. In the last week of his first trip abroad, Emerson made contact with several intellectual luminaries, ones, in particular, which had a significant impact on his intellectual development and subsequent work. In London, he met with John Stuart Mill [1806-1873], who provided him with a calling card of introduction to Thomas Carlyle [1795-1881]. Still in London, he invited himself to see Samuel Taylor Coleridge, who was in his last year of life. The encounter, though disappointing for Coleridge's failure to engage his young admirer, reinforced Emerson's sense that there were many theological issues that no longer held sway over him. Still sensitive to Coleridge's literary prowess, Emerson was sobered by the odd place such concentration on orthodoxy had ultimately led him.

Emerson then sought out Carlyle in Craigenputtock, Scotland. This visit proved immensely more engaging. Emerson was already a keen admirer of Carlyle's rousing critical work, including "The State of German Literature" (1827) and "Sign of the Times" (1829). Unlike his meeting with Coleridge, his time with Carlyle would become the beginning of a long-term friendship and intellectual interaction. In the decades to follow, Emerson became, in essence, Carlyle's American literary agent, helping to channel new works into the mainstream; in 1836 he shepherded Carlyle's *Sartor Resartus* to press (at his own expense); and, in 1839 Emerson edited a four-volume edition of his *Miscellaneous Essays*. Emerson's final celebrity encounter occurred back in London, where he met briefly with William Wordsworth, a poet whose work he had been reading and laboring over since college. The day after the encounter, he departed from Liverpool on his return voyage.

The Anonymous Names Nature

Emerson published his first book anonymously, but it would be the writing that gave him a name. Written in the immediate wake of his return from Europe, and fueled by the tumultuous events that preceded his time abroad, Emerson's narrow book met wide appeal, and signaled a dramatic shift in both his style and the content of his writing. In this work, Emerson's voice is deprived of its usual (ministerial) referent—the Bible. When there are allusions to it, they are suppressed or transmuted. Not required to write sermons, and no longer faced with parishioners seeking guidance from their minister, Emerson's language and the subjects he chose to address were at once liberated from sectarian impositions and the pedagogical urgency that frames (perhaps involuntarily) one's subject, and its exfoliation. The freedom, however, was not used to alienate friends, or to offend former colleagues (though, on occasion, this happened anyway). Instead, the occasion to speak—as it were, nameless and without an overarching guide (viz., the Church)—was employed in the service of conversion. Emerson spent his little book explaining how the world he knew with Ellen and the Church had gone, and how the world he returned to—after Europe—had arrived. He did not dislocate his personal history, or distort his prior tradition. He aimed to explain how they were part of something that exceeded them both, something with far deeper implications, and therefore, far greater potential for invigorating life. *Nature* was the overture that was used to deliver this symphonic message. Emerson began with an assessment of prevailing habits:

23

Our age is retrospective. It builds the sepulchers of the fathers. It writes biographies, histories, criticism. The foregoing generations beheld God and nature face to face; we, through their eyes. Why should we not also enjoy an original relation to the universe? Why should not we have a poetry and philosophy of insight and not of tradition, and a religion by revelation to us, and not the history of theirs? (*EL*, 7)

Emerson was part of this age. He did everything here brought under a critical light. These questions are as much rhetorical incitements as they are admissions to himself (and to others) of habits under suspicion. These first lines, with their confident claims, disclose Emerson's new found orientation: he is no longer looking back, but looking at the present moment. He continues:

. . . The sun shines to-day also. There is more wool and flax in the fields. There are new lands, new men, new thoughts. Let us demand our own works and laws and worship (*Ibid.*).

These sentences mark the revelation that there is potential yet in the world, and that its inhabitants, seized with the proper energy and direction, can transform it as they please—say, into new habits of action. It is as important that we consider what is "new" (that is, what remains to be explored, made, thought) as it is that we consider our possession of it (that is, that we make it "our own"). We may, in fact, wish to appropriate things from the past; but they must be apprehended in an "original relation."

The legitimacy of Emerson's criticisms and commendations, of course, comes from the fact that he used to violate these principles himself: he was beholden to creeds and traditions; he lived in deference to names and histories; he sifted through the "dry bones of the past" for reassurance and inspiration. The error all along was in his object: he was focused, but focused on things that are misleading, corrupting, and soaked with the error of those who have been mislead and corrupted. *Nature*, then, in its eight chapters, is written as an argument for another object of attention.

Emerson works to show that the lessons we seek, or find a need or acknowledge a desire for, are in the natural world. He sustains the temptation that a move to nature (or Nature) may be interpreted as a move to irrationalism, materialism, atheism, and even misanthropism. Yet, nature is not to be our new idol, but a living order of rules and relations reference to which can reinforce human drives and initiatives.

24

Far from constraining us by natural laws, and thus standing in an antagonistic relation to us, nature is taken up as the harbinger of new *human* possibilities.

> But whilst we acquiesce entirely in the permanence of natural laws, the question of the absolute existence of nature still remains open. It is in the uniform effect of culture on the human mind, not to shake our faith in the stability of particular phenomena, as of heat, water, azote; but to lead us to regard nature as a phenomenon, not a substance; to attribute necessary existence to spirit; to esteem nature as an accident and an effect (*EL*, 33).

While Emerson's youth and theological training was sodden by the Calvinist distrust of the body, and denigration of nature, his experience of the death of others, time abroad and at sea, and his apprehension of nature's binding connection to man, made him supersensible to the development of a view that incorporated the body into any defensible view of human life. This development required that our view of nature be revised—seen again—in the light of the belief that neglecting nature was tantamount to denying ourselves. *Nature* is not an ode to atheism, but an incantation of divinity in the natural environment, namely, the world humans inhabit.

> The problem of restoring to the world original and eternal beauty, is solved by the redemption of the soul. The ruin or the blank, that we see when we look at nature, is in our own eye. The axis of vision is not coincident with the axis of things, and so they appear not transparent but opake. The reason why the world lacks unity, and lies broken and in heaps, is, because man is disunited with himself. He cannot be a naturalist, until he satisfies all the demands of the spirit (*EL*, 47).

The priest is blind to nature, and the scientist is blind to spirit. The *naturalist*, however, can see the sanguinity between nature and spirit. The naturalist's study is also prayer. The naturalist's research is both transcendental and immanent.

> . . . [W]hen a faithful thinker, resolute to detach every object from personal relations, and see it in the light of thought, shall, at the same time, kindle science with the fire of the holiest affections, then will God go forth anew into the creation (*Ibid.*).

25

The "God" that arrives is not the god of tradition, but the incarnation of ethics in natural phenomena. The end of the investigation culminates with the recognition—the re-thinking—of truth embodied in bodies and beings, in processes and actions. The naturalist does not write a book to prove this point; it is already published in nature. The naturalist's service comes in helping us to see the presence of this text (already) before us. In this way, the naturalist is akin to a poet.

It has already been illustrated, that every natural process is a version of a moral sentence. The moral law lies at the centre of nature and radiates to the circumference. It is the pith and marrow of every substance, every relation, and every process. All things with which we deal, preach to us. What is a farm but a mute gospel? . . . The moral influence of nature upon every individual is that amount of truth which it illustrates to him (*EL*, 29).

Again, the resonances of Stoic thinking are palpable. Nature is an ethical (as well as a physical and logical) force. Being part of nature means being part of this nexus of confluences. It means taking seriously the ways in which nature informs human conduct. Emerson is turning his attention away from the man-made customs that define and sometimes deny life, and toward a view that nature is *already* moral. The challenge facing us, as Emerson sees it, is to chip away at the blinding crust of tradition that obstructs this vision of nature. A distorted view leads to distorted belief, and therefore to errant behavior. Seeing clearly becomes a prerequisite for living authentically, that is, in accord with nature.

3
Walking in Concord

The year before *Nature* was published, 1835, Emerson bought a house in Concord, Massachusetts where he and his soon-to-be second wife, Lydia would live for the rest of their lives. Emerson called her Lydia*n* to avoid the local accent turning her into Lydia*r*. But how did Emerson, self-divested of his career and therefore an income, and having spent nearly a year abroad traveling, afford to set up a household with Lydian? Inheritance. But from whom?

Ellen Louisa Tucker Emerson, his first wife came from a wealthy family, one from another Concord: Concord, New Hampshire. Upon Ellen's death, Emerson was the beneficiary of a significant amount of money. In the spring of 1834, he received $11,600. The next year he purchased his home for $3,500. By 1837, he had the balance of his inheritance—another $11,400. The inheritance yielded an annual income of around $1,200 dollars. The cost of the Concord home, soon to be dubbed "Bush," gives some sense of how fiscally significant this inheritance was. For further perspective, we might also look ahead ten years, to the account of expenses Henry David Thoreau [1817-1862] gives in *Walden* for goods and services one could purchase in Concord (see the first chapter, "Economy"). It cost Thoreau less than ten dollars to eat for eight months. Even if we grant that the Emersons were eating better, and soon would be feeding more mouths, the inheritance income remains a staggering means of assistance.

A month after *Nature* was published, Emerson's first child, Waldo, was born, taking Emerson's preferred name for himself. A few years later, in 1839, Emerson's second child was born. She was named Ellen Tucker Emerson, after Emerson's first wife.

The inheritance of Ellen's estate made it immediately possible for

Emerson to reasonably consider remaining out of the church. He was, as can be imagined, invited to preach many times (and did so), but he never accepted another clerical post. Furthermore, there was much less pressure for him to consider another profession—say, in law, medicine, or the academy. In the years to come, Emerson would have to supplement his income by giving lectures, but with the publication of *Nature*, he set a precedent for being an independent scholar. This work showed that he could produce influential work outside of an institutional framework, whether that of the church or the university. And this was to his benefit, as in the next two years, he would nearly ensure that he would not be allowed to work in those contexts. "The American Scholar," and "The Divinity School Address" were stunning, radical proclamations—the first a critique of what it means to be(come) educated, the second a trenchant reconsideration of what it means to have faith. Both were received with all the fervor that one might expect when someone questions the relevance of formal education while addressing Phi Beta Kappa at Harvard, and inquires whether God is dead at the nation's most prestigious divinity school.

The American Scholar

A group of graduating seniors at Harvard College, all members of Phi Beta Kappa, invited Emerson to address their class at Cambridge on August 31, 1837. These were young men who had spent the past several years studying books and listening to professors, and now they were on the very cusp of moving on to other prospects—doubtless, promising prospects based on those books and professors. Needless to say, this audience was not representative of America, but it was an exemplification of the community where its best scholars could be found. Emerson's oration on the character and duties of the American scholar, therefore, could not have been better targeted. His news, however, was not taken as a rousing send off. Rather, it was received as an incitement to doubt the solemnity of their educations, and to a concern for what lay ahead—both for America, and for its scholars.

Emerson's immediate invocation is the *American* scholar, conceived as distinct from—what else?—the European scholar. His words bear the heavy influence that his trip to Europe had upon him. He begins, therefore, not with a diagnosis and definition of the American scholar, but with a plea.

. . . Our anniversary is one of hope, and, perhaps, not enough of labor. We do not meet for games of strength or skill, for the recitation of histories, tragedies, and odes, like the ancient Greeks;

28

for parliaments of love and poesy, like the Troubadours; nor for the advancement of science, like our contemporaries in the British and European capitals. Thus far, our holiday has been simply a friendly sign of the survival of the love of letters amongst a people too busy to give to letters any more. As such, it is precious as the sign of an indestructible instinct. Perhaps the time is already come, when it ought to be, and will be, something else; when the sluggard intellect of this continent will look from under its iron lids, and fill the postponed expectation of the world with something better than the exertions of mechanical skill. Our day of dependence, our long apprenticeship to the learning of other lands, draws to a close (*EL*, 53).

The "labor" we have be delinquent in performing is not, as one might expect, "mechanical skill," but *thinking*. But our insufficient labor in this regard was not for idleness; we were quite at work—just on the tracts and treatises from ages and places that do not serve or derive from the America experiment. Indeed, the neglect of our words and thoughts appears an "indestructible instinct." Eventually, the palette will reject these long-standing tastes, and pronounce the development of other ones—ones native, near, and necessary:

The millions, that around us are rushing into life, cannot always be fed on the sere remains of foreign harvests. Events, actions arise, that must be sung, that will sing themselves (*Ibid.*).

Posed as an ancient, famed, and venerable institution, Europe retained an undeniable mystique. It was regarded not only as the de facto origin for so many Americans; it was seen as the proper source of its intellectual attention. Just as the Romans heeded Greece, so should America its cross-Atlantic predecessor. Much of Emerson's exhortation was based on first-hand experience. His long sojourn in Europe, navigating its cities and engaging with its premier scholars, made it seem more like a library than a laboratory. The work had been done. It was already sorted and shelved. While so many young Americans dreamed of Europe as the default authority from which to adopt and to which to adapt, Emerson reckoned that Europe would neither prove the secret to our creative salvation, nor to our progress as a nation—one yet without letters placed after an *American* fashion. We should take our European inheritance seriously, but we should not feel beholden to it. It has much to teach us, yet its lessons must be interpreted for relevance. Emerson had a strategy for mining this

relevance, and for directing us to the production of our own work.
The first delegated task is to see nature as the initial site of instruction. We are to exchange decaying amphitheaters, clogged museums, and soot covered university halls for nature, and by that turn find in its manifestations aspects of ourselves. Thus, whether scientist or school-boy—

> He shall see, that nature is the opposite of the soul, answering to it part for part. One is seal, and one is print. Its beauty is the beauty of his own mind. Its laws are the laws of his own mind. Nature then becomes to him the measure of his attainments. So much of nature as he is ignorant of, so much of his own mind does he not yet possess. And, in fine, the ancient precept, "Know thyself," and the modern precept, "Study nature," become at last one maxim (*EL*, 56).

Emerson both makes a point about scholarship, and shows how it can be done. Here his claims are reinforced—not dictated—by Socrates' command. The quest for self-knowledge remains worth pursuing, but only after being adjusted to the present age. A Stoic might have engendered Emerson's remark two millennia ago, but it is only by the confirmation of a modern mind that the prior teaching takes shape for present purposes.
The admonition to create for one's own time is never more apparent than when addressing another of the influences that mold the human mind, namely, books.

> Each age, it is found, must write its own books; or rather, each generation for the next succeeding. The books of an older period will not fit this (*EL*, 56-7).

What is more, we are capable of writing our own books—our own letters. The address at hand is part of that project, at once a scene of instruction and lesson of reception. Emerson estimates that it is only the "active soul" who can express "genius"—and every one has this potential (*EL*, 57). As things stand, however, many scholars are not inspired to speak what they think.

> . . . [T]he scholar is the delegated intellect. In the right state, he is, *Man Thinking*. In the degenerate state, when the victim of society, he tends to become a mere thinker, or, still worse, the parrot of other men's thinking (*EL*, 54. Emerson's italics).

30

Being a scholar does not mean just knowing what *others* think, but also what one thinks. The scholar, as Man Thinking, is inspired by what he reads, not disparaged by it. The ideas may be profound, the arguments well rendered, but that does not entail the end of scholarship. Being discouraged by books, oddly enough, leads us to venerate them. We cannot find our own words, so we cherish the ones already put in place. The office of scholar is vacated.

The sacredness which attaches to the act of creation,—the act of thought,—is transferred to the record. The poet chanting, was felt to be a divine man: henceforth the chant is divine also. The writer was a just and wise spirit: henceforward it is settled, the book is perfect; as love of the hero corrupts into worship of his statue. Instantly, the book becomes noxious: the guide is a tyrant. The sluggish and perverted mind of the multitude, slow to open to the incursions of Reason, having once so opened, having once received this book, stands upon it, and makes an outcry, if it is disparaged. Colleges are built on it. Books are written on it by thinkers, not by Man Thinking; by men of talent, that is, who start wrong, who set out from accepted dogmas, not from their own sight of principles. Meek young men grow up in libraries, believing it their duty to accept the views, which Cicero, which Locke, which Bacon, have given, forgetful that Cicero, Locke, and Bacon were only young men in libraries, when they wrote these books.

Hence, instead of Man Thinking, we have the bookworm (*EL*, 57).

"Reason" is being used here in the way that those influenced by Coleridge used it—that is, as that which exhibits one's truest insights, one's most honest impulses. Reason is contrasted with Understanding, the latter of which registers the results of technical or analytical thinking. The scholar blind to his or her own intuitions of Reason is, therefore, merely a cataloguer of thinking done by others.

The third foundational influence on the scholar is action (nature and books being the first two). Emerson struggled with the long-standing perception, and his own doubt, that to be a scholar—to fitfully nourish one's intellect—one had to neglect the rest of life. Whether figured as the reclusive monk, the cosmopolitan clergy, or the college professor, there is the suspicion that one's body, and one's social health is compromised by too much study. Emerson is quick to ratify this concern, countering the image of disengaged mind by identifying

31

action as "essential" to its vitality (and therefore to the character of what one thinks).

Inaction is cowardice, but there can be no scholar without the heroic mind. The preamble of thought, the transition through which it passes from the unconscious to the conscious, is action. Only so much do I know, as I have lived. Instantly we know whose words are loaded with life, and whose not (*EL*, 60).

It were as if the oxygen in one's blood, raised by physical exertion, were somehow translated into the words one writes, showing them painted with a healthy rouge spurred by a movement that compensates for the pale blonde inertness of the page. The book itself becomes a body born from action, from the scholar's involvement with the world beyond its limits. Everything in one's life becomes relevant to one's expression, both in its form and content. There is no other way to forge this sanguine connection.

If it were only for a vocabulary, the scholar would be covetous of action. Life is our dictionary. Years are well spent in country labors; in town,—in the insight into trades and manufactures, in frank intercourse with many men and women; in science; in art; to the one end of mastering in all their faces a language by which to illustrate and embody our perceptions. I learn immediately from any speaker how much he has already lived, through the poverty or the splendor of his speech. Life lies behind us as the quarry from whence we get tiles and copestones for the masonry of to-day. This is the way to learn grammar. Colleges and books only copy the language which the field and the work-yard made (*EL*, 61-2).

Scholarship does not require one's withdrawal from the world, rather the inverse. For it is in an intimate engagement with the multifarious and unstable factors that frame everyday life that one builds a vocabulary with which to speak. Emerson revises our notion of *reading*—extending it beyond the classroom and the library, spreading it to include the texts that comprise our wider experience of the world. The grammar of experience, Emerson presumes, yields better insight than the coveted handbooks that too quickly define the curriculum of thought, and therefore, the boundaries of expression.

Nature, books, and action influence the scholar, which is to say, they educate her. But such instruction is not merely for the writing of books, it is so that she may come to realize her own power as Man

Thinking. Emerson calls this power "self-trust." A few years later, he will develop this notion and call it "self-reliance." This may seem an odd conclusion: Why should one's training as an American scholar culminate in self-trust? Why not, for example, the composition of an admirable book? Because once sensitized to the language of the world, the scholar risks being swallowed by the opinions of others. So perceptive is the scholar that she fears she cannot speak without provoking scorn or causing offense. Self-trust is the kind of intellectual courage the scholar must practice in order to create in the light of her experience. Experience is the prerequisite for creative intuition, but self-trust transforms such interior insights into expression, namely, as tuition.

> These being his functions, it becomes him to feel all confidence in himself, and to defer never to the popular cry. He and he only knows the world. . . . Let him not quit his belief that a popgun is a popgun, though the ancient and honorable of the earth affirm it to be the crack of doom. In silence, in steadiness, in severe abstraction, let him hold by himself. . . . He then learns, that in going down into the secrets of his own mind, he has descended into the secrets of all minds (*EL*, 67).

The scholar's work is not incidental, but substantial, and is pursued ever with high stakes and palpable hazards. That is how it must be, otherwise we make the great risk, and in turn take the greater loss, of disowning ourselves from the world we inhabit. Emerson taunts us to avoid this attitude:

> Yes, we are the cowed,—we the trustless. It is a mischievous notion that we are come late into nature; that the world was finished a long time ago. As the world was plastic and fluid in the hands of God, so it is ever to so much of his attributes as we bring to it. To ignorance and sin, it is flint (*EL*, 65).

Emerson's audience that late summer day was mainly teenagers, and it was they who invited him to speak. These were, to be sure, talented and restless young men, and Emerson's words recognized both their position and their disposition. As Emerson illustrated what an American scholar might be, he did so as an American scholar himself. In the aftermath of his oration, however, no aspiring scholar could justify merely saying what Emerson had said. The American scholar had to learn what *he* could say. And then *say* it.

33

We must become, Emerson commended, new agents of thought—working out our own relation to nature, books, and action. In "The American Scholar," Emerson, writes a critique and a meta-critique of the American scholar, for even as he is writing about what such a figure could be, he is making an example of it through his writing. The paradox of his lesson is that we cannot merely adopt what he says, treating him as *the* touchstone—otherwise we become dogmatists of an American (instead of a European) tradition. The affirmation of his voice, as much as the evasion of our own voice, would therein leave us out of touch. Using Emerson this way renders his lesson benign even as it at implicates us as untouchable (both unable to sense his invocation and complacent in a mood beyond reproach). Therefore, the skepticism of scholarship and the confidence of the scholar must be asserted in order for a critical evolution in American thinking to transpire. Nearing this, we no longer find ourselves thinking European thoughts or American thoughts. We realize ourselves as Man Thinking.

Address at the Divinity School in Cambridge

On July 15, 1838, in the Chapel at Divinity Hall on the floor just above where he lived while a student at Harvard Divinity School in the mid-1820's, Emerson delivered an address that would arouse the attention of his alma mater, his native city, and soon, the national community. The attention, much of it cast defensively and with an impression of offense, was provoked by Emerson's critical look at the culture of faith, including both the institutions of religion and the habits of believers.

Emerson's radical moment at the podium in Divinity Hall was neither received as a blithe interpretive gesture, nor as a series of idiosyncratic rantings from an alumnus returning to offer constructive criticism. By this time, Emerson's role as a scholar and public figure was becoming better known. There seemed few pretensions that he would take up another clerical position, and after the publication of *Nature*, few could deny that his comprehension of Christianity was significantly disjointed from even the most liberal of the already liberal Unitarian mainstream. In those days, Unitarianism was the dominant denomination of Christianity at Harvard. Emerson's remarks to the small group gathered in the chapel were explicit in their critiques of the local incarnations of religiosity, and the wider, historical line that defined Christianity.

Soon after he spoke, Emerson was seen as a threat of the highest caliber and sophistication. He spoke with such eloquence and

34

efficiency that his very own teachers, not to mention the coterie of graduating students, were shocked and disturbed by the impendence of the interrogation they heard. This appraisal is not easily over-dramatized, even from our vantage, as the immediate effects upon him were palpable and lasting. Emerson's words were not thickly veiled, so it is perhaps unsurprising that he was not invited back to Harvard again until he was in his sixties, nearly thirty years after he gave the address. In 1866, in what may be read as an act of contrition, Harvard awarded him an honorary Doctor of Laws degree. While America had embraced him with increasing vigilance, year after year beginning in 1836, Harvard declined to acknowledge his significance until late in his life. How much easier it is to celebrate the already celebrated. And it was not until after his death that Harvard began to fully reclaim him—naming the hall that houses the philosophy department after him (1900), later, putting up a passage from his journals at the entry gate to Harvard Yard (placed there, the selection becomes tinged with irony), and hanging a plaque of recognition in the Chapel at the Divinity School (that, with dismay, misquotes him)—invoking Emerson's presence as perhaps one of its signature alumni, and drawing from one of its most noted scholars with great ease and frequency, especially at moments of wide exposure, such as at graduations, convocations, and dedications.

Emerson occupied a transitional point in the history of American religious experience: he bore witness to a private and a wider cultural shift from a Calvinistic and Puritan worldview dominated by inherited religious and ethical dogma to a political and scientific secularism that grew in popularity and strength as the nineteenth century burned on. His own life bears evidence of this shift, say from his early days under the instruction and influence of his Calvinist aunt Mary Moody Emerson to his young adult life when, in Paris, he affirmed that he wanted to be "a naturalist." The address delivered at the Divinity School in Cambridge can be read as a record of this shift in Emerson, and his estimation of this shift in America. Emerson did not see this transformation as a form of "infidelity," but rather, the proper way in which the individual can come to a consciousness of authentic faith. His words, therefore, reinforce and catalyze further the change (in himself and in a broader company of believers).

The scandalousness of Emerson's address did not reside, as one might think, in heralding the death of God, and thus the end of Christianity's relevance (though he queries that his peers often behave "as if God were dead" (*EL*, 83)). Indeed, the issue was quite the inverse, and so, that much more scathing. Emerson conceived that it

35

was Christianity itself, and its many permutations including the widely prominent influence of Calvinism in New England, that had done away with God. Christianity, which celebrates the divinity of Jesus and the inspired words of Scripture, depotentiates all time to follow by devaluing it, and degrading those who inhabit it. In the aftermath of Christ's crucifixion, and the inscription of the Bible, it were as if the world could no longer be the site of miracles and creation.

Emerson's message was misunderstood by many. They heard in his words an anti-Christian atheism. But he was speaking, in fact, of just the opposite, namely, a form of religious feeling that allowed one to perceive divinity as a *present* experience. God's presence is not something lost in the past, the privilege of an ancient world and old words. Rather, God is immanent, within each of us.

At present, Emerson lamented, "The evils of the church that now are manifest" (*EL*, 91). These evils are peculiar, for they are evils of omission, not commission. It is that the church has stagnated, and in the process anesthetized its constituency, which makes its offenses so offensive. Christians have, as it were, died at church.

> The stationariness of religion; the assumption that the age of inspiration is past, that the Bible is closed; the fear of degrading the character of Jesus by representing him as a man; indicate with sufficient clearness the falsehood of our theology (*EL*, 88).

Emerson contends that there are "Two inestimable advantages Christianity has given us," first, the Sabbath, and secondly, preaching. This opinion should have arrived warmly on the ears of those ministers-in-training sitting before Emerson in the Chapel at Divinity Hall. And yet, they might also have been disparaged to hear Emerson say that these are the "two errors" of religious life as now practiced.

Emerson surmises that "Historical Christianity has fallen into the error that corrupts all attempts to communicate religion" (*EL*, 81). This corruption is evidenced in the way that the faithful are beholden to keeping the habits of faith that they received from family and church. In this position, there is no reason to believe that anything more than stale discourse is possible. Once I know to which church you belong, I may close my ears, for I know what you will say before you say it. A few years later Emerson will say: "If I know your sect, I anticipate your argument" (*EL*, 264). In this way, historical Christianity has both embalmed human imagination and veiled the possibility of individual religious expression.

These criticisms are predicated on the belief that man possesses what Emerson calls "the sentiment of virtue" (*EL*, 76). It is variously described as a "moral sentiment" and a "religious sentiment," but there remains a common feature: the perception of divinity within oneself. This is described as "a reverence and delight in the presence of certain divine laws" and "an insight of the perfection of the laws of the soul" (*Ibid.*). The unmistakable implication is that one need look no further than one's own soul to embrace God. "If a man is at heart just, then in so far is he God" (*Ibid.*). It is historical Christianity, Emerson insists, that has blinded us to the presence of this sentiment, and thus, to the presence of God. It is this sentiment that reveals how "a man is made the Providence to himself" and that "God incarnates himself in man" (*EL*, 77, 80).

The second error of religious practice is seen in the "vulgar tone of preaching" (*EL*, 82). Everyone, not just ministers, has "come to speak of the revelation as somewhat long ago given and done, as if God were dead" (EL, 83). The second error is stacked upon the first: if we have men who are mere parrots of antiquity, who are numb to their (own) sentiments, and to the immanence of divinity (in them), what can be hoped for in their speech? How could such desperation preach inspiration?

> The spirit only can teach. Not any profane man, not any sensual, not any liar, not any slave can teach, but only he can give, who has; he only can create, who is. The man on whom the soul descends, through whom the soul speaks, alone can teach (*Ibid.*).

But one cannot teach if one is not alive. Preachers have become habituated to creeds, and in that adaptation have deformed themselves, and as it turns out—the lessons they seek to convey to others.

> Faith makes us, and not we it, and faith makes its own forms. All attempts to contrive a system are as cold as the new worship introduced by the French to the goddess of Reason,—to-day, pasteboard and fillagree, and ending to-morrow in madness and murder. Rather let the breath of new life be breathed by you through the forms already existing. For, if once you are alive, you shall find they shall become plastic and new. The remedy to their deformity is first, soul, and second, soul, and evermore, soul. A whole popedom of forms, one pulsation of virtue can uplift and vivify (*EL*, 91).

When Emerson said this, we can imagine that it did not arrive as a strategy for resuscitation, but a recipe for hyperventilation. These are, indeed, deep breaths. And Emerson himself was making them, and taking them. As in "The American Scholar," the occasion at the podium is reinforced by its double performance—one heard in the words, the other shown in the actor. Emerson is, in short, preaching to others how he wishes to be preached to. Even if the preacher can come back to life—be reborn, out of a difficult labor—it is not enough to dictate one's new faith. Such tuition is always supplementary to intuition. One cannot *teach* another how to honor his or her sentiment.

> It cannot be received at second hand. Truly speaking, it is not instruction, but provocation, that I can receive from another soul. . . . [T]he absence of this primary faith is the presence of degradation (*EL*, 79).

God appears dead to us because we have cinched the channels through which we might receive Him. The preacher has distracted us from this fact by reiterating the history of Christianity, with its stories of how God once came to earth but is now vanished. Emerson leans upon Jesus to show "what a distortion did his doctrine and memory suffer in the same, in the next, and the following ages!"

> He said, in this jubilee of sublime emotion, 'I am divine. Through me, God acts; through me, speaks. Would you see God, see me; or, see thee, when thou also thinkest as I now think' (*EL*, 80).

Have our preachers preached *this*? "[C]hurches are not built on his principles, but on his tropes," and so the literal lesson here was lost in the mire of metaphor. The audience of Christianity has been denied preachers who speak not from books, but from their souls. ". . . [T]he man who aims to speak as books enable, as synods use, as the fashion guides, and as interest commands, babbles. Let him hush" (*EL*, 83).

"Preaching is the expression of the moral sentiment in application to the duties of life" (*EL*, 84). The preacher, like the scholar, is charged with a simple, but painful, task: to expose the character of his or her life to others. The standard, however, is to find the preacher cowed behind the lives of others. The preacher's lesson, again and again reinforced, is that we ought to remain in deference, and never indifferent, to past voices because ours are not worth making audible. When we hear the preacher, we do not hear him, but what stands *behind* him. Our preachers have become transparent—ghosts

ministering on behalf of ancient creeds—as invisible as they are
lifeless.

> Whenever the pulpit is usurped by a formalist, then is the
> worshipper defrauded and disconsolate. We shrink as soon as the
> prayers begin, which do not uplift, but smite and offend us. . . . I
> once heard a preacher who sorely tempted me to say, I would go to
> church no more. . . . A snow storm was falling around us. The
> snow storm was real; the preacher merely spectral; and the eye felt
> the sad contrast in looking at him, and then out of the window
> behind him, into the beautiful meteor of the snow (*EL*, 84).

There is a double criticism here. Snowflakes are all snow. But, we are
told, no two snowflakes are identical. Emerson can therefore admire
the snow because its members fall neatly as a unity, *and* as particulars.
There is a context (the storm), and there is an incident of discrete
expression (the flake). The more obvious criticism drawn by this
metaphor, however, lies in the moral performance of the snow: it is not
ashamed to be itself. The single flake bears its uniqueness even as it
contributes to the wider historical process that will soon bury it. It is a
fleeting life, to be sure, but it sustains itself. The preacher does not
show his design.

> He had lived in vain. He had no one word intimating that he had
> laughed or wept, was married or in love, had been commended, or
> cheated, or chagrined. If he had ever lived and acted, we were
> none the wiser for it. . . . (*EL*, 84-5).

As an astute diagnostician, Emerson also levied a remedy for the
malaise that so desperately crippled his former profession. To his
young audience, he said:

> Let me admonish you, first of all, to go alone; to refuse the
> good models, even those which are sacred in the imagination of
> men, and dare to love God without mediator or veil. . . . Thank
> God for these good men, but say, 'I also am a man.' Imitation
> cannot go above its model. The imitator dooms himself to
> hopeless mediocrity (*EL*, 88-9).

Emerson is giving advice he has already taken himself. He has been
the preacher that he now so sorely laments: "Alas for the unhappy man
that is called to stand in the pulpit, and *not* give bread of life" (*EL*, 86).

Generation after generation, we are told that emulation will reinforce us, and will justify us to others. But it is precisely this "soul-destroying slavery to habit," to the habituated models of men, that so defames and deforms us in our duties (*EL*, 89). The "true preacher," Emerson counters, ". . . deals out to the people his life,—life passed through the fire of thought" (*EL*, 85). Training has made the person and the personal seem delinquent and irrelevant, as if the presence of a person were sacrilegious. "Christianity destroys the power of preaching, by withdrawing it from the exploration of the moral nature of man, where the sublime is, where are the resources of astonishment and power" (*EL*, 86).

In these two errors—the corrosive and compromising influence of historical Christianity, and the fraudulence and frailty of the office of preaching—Emerson sees the "causes of a decaying church and a wasting unbelief" (*EL*, 87). Of these results, he asks: "And what greater calamity can fall upon a nation, than the loss of worship?" (*Ibid.*). Emerson is neither calling for the dismantling of the church, nor for the dismissal of its ministers. Indeed, the pronouncement is just the opposite. He speaks to provoke in his hearers the idea that a new inhabitation of habit must occur. To revitalize faith, one must be willing to donate a *living* truth. "What hinders that now, everywhere," Emerson queries in the last few lines of his address, ". . . wherever the invitation of men or your own occasions lead you, you speak the very truth, as your life and conscience teach it, and cheer the waiting, fainting hearts of men with new hope and new revelation?" (*EL*, 91).

The Sabbath and preaching, therefore, are crucial to the rehabilitation of man. We have been fooled by our buildings and our books to see in them the end of our attention. Statues and sacraments have been taken as the appropriate objects of worship. But *we* are alive, not they. If life is to be given, we must give it.

And now, my brothers, you will ask, What in these desponding days can be done by us? The remedy is already declared in the ground of our complaint of the Church. We have contrasted the Church with the Soul. In the soul, then, let the redemption be sought. Wherever a man comes, there comes revolution. The old is for slaves. When a man comes, all books are legible, all things transparent, all religions are forms (*EL*, 88).

In giving a sermon, in making use of the Church, the soul should be preached. Emerson looks for "the new Teacher." "Now man is ashamed of himself; he skulks and sneaks through the world, to be tolerated, to be pitied. . ." (*EL*, 87). Instruction from the soul, provocation by preachers sensitive to their divine capacities, will not, by reaction, teach pride, intolerance, or indifference. All the more, heeding the soul will be a guard against both extremes.

It is the office of a true teacher to show us that God is, not was; that He speaketh, not spake. The true Christianity,—a faith like Christ's in the infinitude of man,—is lost (*EL*, 88).

The remedy to decay and waste—and to this lost Christianity—is in regaining the alienated orientation to individual, human power. Christ, a "true" teacher as the "new" teacher, returns us to ourselves, forcing a faith that is grounded on the infinity of the individual. "None assayeth the stern ambition to be the Self of the nation, and of nature, but each would be an easy secondary to some Christian scheme, or sectarian connection, or some eminent man" (*Ibid.*). In a newfound confidence, we are apprised of a primary status hitherto exiled by habits of subjugation and self-denial. We do not have to be *like* Christ—God made incarnate—because we *are* him already.

Pathway through Woods to Worlds and Words

From his adolescence, Emerson made a habit of walking long distances, most of the time in companionship. Forged early, this habit proved to be an important aspect of Emerson's sense of human vitality and creativity. Walking was treated as both a useful and sometimes a necessary elixir for thinking. The movement of the body, the crossing of terrain, signaled a movement of thought—where covering topics resembled ambulating over topographies.

When he was twenty, in August 1823, Emerson took a walking trip to the Connecticut Valley and climbed Mt. Holyoke. At this point, the outing had the character of adventure and exploration. During these months, his private journals began to swell, filling with remarks on his diet of reading, which ranged from the Stoics (Seneca, Ovid, Lucretius) to Madame de Staël.

At the beginning of the next decade, after his first wife Ellen died, his habit adapted. For months on end, he walked to her grave in Roxbury. His journals measure his contemplation on this loss, mainly in verse.

Soon after, in 1833, his journals became the site of remarks from his walks in Italy, France, and England—walks through Roman ruins, within Parisian museums, and beside Carlyle in Scotland.

As Emerson settled into life in Concord, he began to use walking as much for its influence on his body as for its potential to provoke thinking. To this end, he would often invite friends and neighbors with him as he walked through the woods, including the land he owned at Walden Pond.

Caroline Sturgis, Margaret Fuller, and Henry Thoreau were frequent walking partners, especially as he made a turn into the 1840's, a decade that would see the production of another installment of influential writing. In an effort to develop his friendship with Nathaniel Hawthorne (who came to live in the Emerson family home, thereafter renamed The Old Manse), Emerson recommended that they embark on a trip to see the Shakers in Harvard, Massachusetts. Hawthorne obliged, and the two made the forty-mile walk (to and from) in two days (Richardson, 376).

> Our walk had no incidents. It needed none, for we were in excellent spirits, had much conversation, for we were both old collectors who had never had opportunity before to show each other our cabinets, so that we could have filled with matter much longer days (September 27, 1842. *J*, vol. VII, 272-3).

One of his most consistent walking partners was the poet William Ellery Channing II (son of William Ellery Channing, the Unitarian minister). It is some measure of Emerson's esteem for walking (and for Channing) that Emerson recommended that he pull together some remarks on walking into a book—to be entitled *Concord Walking* (Richardson, 515). It would be a collaboration, drawn mainly from Emerson's journals and what Channing would want to contribute, much as their many walks together were a collaboration. The book would be a record, to some degree, of that ambulatory conversation, and their remarks on the capacious topic of walking and thinking. The book never materialized. But the project, one stoked by Emerson, indicates his keenness both for walking and for the effect it has on one's relationships with others and one's writing. As Emerson wrote to Caroline Sturgis about a recent visit from Channing: ". . . [W]e wandered over much land & many topics" (August 5, 1842. *L*, vol. VII, 506). The geographical topography is covered in parallel with cognitive *topoi*. The mantra might have been: walk and talk. After an excursion with Channing to White Pond, in Concord, Emerson wrote of his walking partner:

> Yesterday, 28 October, another walk with Ellery well worth commemoration if that were possible; but no pen could write what

we saw: it needs the pencils of all the painters that ever existed, to aid the description. . . . In walking with Ellery you shall always see what was never before shown to the eye of man (October 29, 1848. *J*, vol. XI, 36, 38).

But Emerson did not just write about walking in his journals. He also made ample use of walking in his public, published writing. From his first lectures to his last books, Emerson found in walking a dynamic activity that served as a powerful symbol for cognitive life and the proper proportions of human engagement with the world. It speaks well, therefore, of Emerson's esteem for walking to find him quoting Rousseau (whose final book was *Reveries of the Solitary Walker*): "Walking has the best value as gymnastics for the mind. . . . 'Walking,' said Rousseau, 'has something which animates and vivifies my ideas'" (*CW*, vol. XII, 141-2). It is all the more dispiriting, one might say, and Emerson *does* say, that "Few men know how to take a walk" (*CW*, vol. XII, 142). It is not far, nor unfair, to say that few know how to think. These references highlight Emerson's persistent use of walking as literally bound up with the fitness of the mind, and as a metaphor for the continuity of cognitive and physical powers.

If Emerson had distinguished aspirations for the influence of walking upon thinking, he was also sober about the limitations that bind us in all directions. And he was sensitive to other sorts of limitations—not just cognitive, but perceptual, not solely imaginative but temporal. One can surmise this, for example, in his dominant use of visual metaphor. So, while walking should enable "divine illumination" and "intercourse with the spiritual world," it can often merely muddle (*CW*, vol. I, 227). Thus his concern in his *First Series* essay "Intellect."

> Our spontaneous action is always the best. You cannot with your best deliberation and heed come so close to any question as your spontaneous glance shall bring you, whilst you rise from your bed, or walk abroad in the morning after meditating the matter before sleep on the previous night. Our thinking is a pious reception (*CW*, vol. II, 328).

While walking can prove a helpful elixir, and on occasion a necessary tonic to thinking, it can also be an opiate—deliberation can, as it were, be too deliberate. This condition is partly inherent and partly produced.

Emerson's concern both for individual integrity and for social interaction often finds its voice in a critique of one's use of one's eyes,

Those who are not self-possessed obtrude and pain us. . . .
They fear to offend, they bend and apologize, and walk through
life with a timid step (*CW*, vol. VI, 186).

Instead of posture, we have posturing, as in "Self-Reliance," twenty
years earlier, where Emerson parodies the same: "Man is timid and
apologetic; he is no longer upright. . . . He is ashamed before the blade
of grass or the blowing rose" (*EL*, 270). In one's meekness and
sycophantic habits, one becomes distorted—monstrous.

The state of society is one in which the members have suffered
amputation from the trunk, and strut about so many walking
monsters,—a good finger, a neck, a stomach, an elbow, but never a
man (*CW*, vol. I, 83).

In an amputated condition, one is deprived the confidence that comes
with unity. Our timidity seems both a cause and an effect of our
dislocation and deformity. We ". . . walk ever with reverted eyes, like
those monsters who look backwards" (*CW*, vol. II, 126). It is no
wonder, then, that the *first* line of Emerson's published career reads:
"Our age is retrospective" (*EL*, 7). When looking back, one cannot see,
but merely leer, one cannot walk, but only bend and sway.

But man postpones or remembers; he does not live in the present,
but with reverted eye laments the past, or, heedless of the riches
that surround him, stands on tiptoe to foresee the future (*EL*, 270).

Looking back, requires an unnatural contortion, and so disables one
from walking as one might, as one should: with head (and eyes) facing
forward and posture upright. Emerson reminds us, as if we had
forgotten (or did not notice): "the eyes of man are set in his forehead,
not in his hindhead" (*EL*, 90).

When we face our friends, we face them eye to eye. And when we
walk beside them, we walk with eyes to the landscape before us. The
rarity of good friends may be attributed to a failure to see the influence
of these images, that is, to see how walking (literally and
tropologically) puts us in a dignified relation to others. Concerning our
friendships, Emerson writes:

We walk alone in the world. Friends such as we desire are dreams and fables. . . . Our impatience betrays us into rash and foolish alliances which no god attends. By persisting in your path, though you forfeit the little you gain the great. You demonstrate yourself, so as to put yourself out of the reach of false relations, and you draw to you the first-born of the world,—those rare pilgrims whereof only one or two wander in nature at once. . . (*CW*, vol. II, 213).

It is thus the *path* one *walks* that brings one into communion with those who *wander*. Ontologically speaking, we walk alone. It is a profound achievement of one's genius to make this empirically otherwise, that is, to find a friend, to have someone to walk beside.

On April 19, 1882, Emerson took his last walk. Aged seventy-eight, he went out by himself and was a caught in the rain. Two days later, he was diagnosed with pneumonia. And on April twenty-seventh, Emerson was stilled.

The Lyceum, not the Academy

Emerson occupies a developing role in American cultural life, what we might call that of a public intellectual or a cultural critic. These titles seem fitting in so far as he is neither a religious leader, nor an academic. He inhabits a sort of middle position, enabling and encouraging thinking between dyads—between the dogmatic preacher and the institutional professor. Religiosity is reconceived as a mode of seeing, and not a mode of believing. "As I am, so I see" (*EL*, 489). And theoretical arguments are turned to the everyday. Emerson is not religious in a traditional sense because of his suspicion of and distance from dogma. And he is not secular in a pure way because he infuses his conceptual framework with divine attributes. Emerson's natural theology occasionally edges close to pantheism (that God is omnipresent in phenomena), or even animism (that consciousness persists through all of nature). But these views fail to capture the peculiar and promising capacities of the human. Pantheism and animism are too democratic; they reduce life to one level. The human is natural, but it is *also* cultural. For this reason, Emerson's view hinges as importantly on natural history as it does on cultural anthropology. To speak of the human requires contact with the human.

After Aristotle, Emerson's peripatetics greatly inform both the content and the performance of his philosophical exercises. As a Stoic orator or a member of Aristotle's Lyceum might, Emerson proclaimed himself to others, and moved from place to place between such presentations. Unlike the ancient Lyceum, however, the Lyceum

Circuit did not impose an institutional framework upon its participants. Emerson was, in modern sports parlance, a free-agent, or in current business terms, a consultant. He was hired for a season. There was no tenure, no academic line to tow, no school to speak on behalf of. Emerson was his own review committee: he spoke his latent conviction (*EL*, 259).

The flexible conditions that allowed Emerson to speak as he wished show only one side of the affair. The other side, of course, is the audience. As a minister, one's audience comes to one's house of worship, and knows whence one speaks. As a professor, one's audience arrives at one's house of inquiry, and knows the angle from which one approaches the subject. But Emerson went out in search of his audience. And when he arrived before them, neither knew the other. The audience awaited what this man would say. And Emerson addressed his audience assured of its diversities and differences, that it was not a monolithic ear, but was a heterogeneous conglomeration of citizens. How different does "Man the Reformer" (1841) sound knowing it was delivered before the Mechanics' Apprentices Library Association? Does thinking of the crowd at the Mercantile Library Association change one's reception of "The Young American" (1844)? Emerson, of course, knew whether he would be addressing the senior class at Harvard College (as he did in 1837) or an informally gathered society of mechanics; why then do his essays, lectures, and addresses not betray this difference? How can it be that Emerson's voice remains steady regardless of who stands before him? It is not because he is incapable of variation, but because he sees no *need* for variation. One does not have to speak up to one group and down to another. One need not select a different vocabulary to elicit attention from one party and shift to another set of words to engage another. Emerson's peripatetics moves him from venue to venue, but while the scenes and senses of his audience change, he abides by his words.

Being a public intellectual or a cultural critic in the mid-nineteenth century did not entail televised talk shows, aggressively publicized book tours, and live Internet webcasts. Emerson's inhabitation of the role, however, gives us a sense of how he interpreted it. Surely, lecturing was a paying job, and that mattered. But it is in Emerson's outreach to America, his attempt to infiltrate its demographic landscape that becomes more relevant. To be a proper critic of America, one had to *see* it and *say* it—see America and then say to Americans what had been seen. Emerson's anthropological criticism was not hatched by a hermit's supposition, or extrapolated from a provincial community. It was earned by going into the distended realm under consideration—the city and the country; the market and the farm; the college and the play field; the bar and the intellectual society. Emerson's mobility of body—his travels and travails—proved to engender mobility in his writings. They travel well across America because they are, in large measure, drawn from his responses to it. And while they were widely well-received in his time, how can we account for their continued relevance? Perhaps it is that the enduring importance of Emerson's prose is in some way derived from his habit of walking, his practice of going forth, his willingness to remain unsettled. His writings possess these features in so far as they continue to speak to us, and yet elude our attempts to secure a final or fixed lesson from them.

Thoreau, Bachelor of Thought and Nature

Emerson first met Henry David Thoreau in 1837, when Emerson was thirty-three, and Thoreau was just graduating from Harvard College, aged twenty. The two developed a friendship based as much on intellectual as physical vigor, since many of their conversations occurred while walking together in the woods of Concord. Walden Pond was a familiar mark on their pathways, and Emerson would, several years later, grant Thoreau permission to build his hut on its shore. Thoreau's time on the land, at the Pond, from 1845 to 1847 is given account in his *Walden; or, Life in the Woods* (1854).

In the early 1840's, Thoreau became a familiar presence at the Emerson household—sharing meals, helping with chores, and playing with the children. In August 1847, a month after Emerson had been invited to give a series of lectures in England, Lidian invited Thoreau—still living at Walden Pond—to move in with the family during Emerson's second trip abroad. A week later, he brought his two year, two month, and two day experiment to a close; and shortly thereafter, accepted Lidian's invitation.

Emerson's nearly year-long absence gave him another chance to become saturated with English culture, and to develop further an in-person (instead of epistolary) connection with Carlyle. And it was in the wake of this trip that Emerson began to gather notes for what would become *English Traits*.

Once returned to Concord, however, Emerson found Thoreau had grown comfortable, perhaps too comfortable, spending time with the children, and especially with Lidian. The reorientation back to domestic life proved to be difficult, and for a while sent a wedge between the friendship. Fortunately, the tensions and traumas were short-lived as when Thoreau, at age forty-four, died in May 1862, the friends had long since reconciled (Richardson, ch. 78, *passim*.).

Emerson admired many things about his friend, not the least of which was Thoreau's will to renounce what did not fit him—whether taking up a profession, or eating meat; whether paying taxes or getting married. But Emerson was equally impressed by what he adopted: his habit of walking (absent scientific instruments or technical field guides) that made him seem a paragon of the naturalist. He was, as Emerson eulogized, "the bachelor of thought and Nature" (*EP*, 399).

Ever dogged by illnesses, or by the memory of their doggedness, Emerson appreciated Thoreau's robust physicality—his ability to live *in* his body; and his perception that bodily virtue was a necessary requisite for literary and philosophical insight: "The length of his walk uniformly made the length of his writing. If shut up in the house, he did not write at all" (*EP*, 402). And Emerson thought it "a pleasure and a privilege to walk with him" (*EP*, 405).

It must be counted that Emerson lamented that his deepest admiration and affection for his younger friend could not be shared by many others, partly on account of Thoreau's behavior, and partly because of his premature death. With self-conscious and unashamed selfishness, Emerson admitted how he wished Thoreau would have been better known to the wider world when he was alive.

> . . . I so much regret the loss of his rare powers of action, that I cannot help counting it a fault in him that he had no ambition. Wanting this, instead of engineering for all America, he was the captain of a huckleberry party. Pounding beans is good to the end of pounding empires one of these days; but if, at the end of years, it is still only beans! (*EP*, 409).

Thoreau *did* have ambition, just not of a conventional sort, and for this his "art of living well," "refusals," "genius," "patience," "conviction of the indifferency of all places," "whim," "love of the Indian," "spiritual perception," "absolute religion," "holy living," and "solitude" were deprived to so many who could have benefited from an encounter with him. And all this for the worst since, Emerson estimated that "No truer American existed than Thoreau" (*EP*, 401).

> The country knows not yet, or in the least part, how great a son it has lost. It seems an injury that he should leave in the midst of his broken task, which none else can finish,—a kind of indignity to so noble a soul, that it should depart out of Nature before yet he has been really shown to his peers for what he is (*EP*, 410-1).

48

By the time Thoreau died, Emerson knew "how great a son" he had lost in his Waldo. For America, losing Thoreau was losing such a boy—brilliant, rare, and irreplaceable.

The Dial *with Margaret Fuller*

In the summer of 1836, as Emerson was finishing his first book, *Nature*, he welcomed Margaret Fuller for a three-week visit. The intellectual stimulus she provided would help him not only complete his book to some satisfaction, but become a near-constant presence in the next decade of his work. Her accomplished translation of Goethe's *Tasso* was Emerson's initial exposure to her. But it would be their conversations and collaborations, and her pivotal book, *Women in the Nineteenth Century*, that sustained their intellectual engagement and emotional connection. If Fuller affected the arc of *Nature* by drawing its conclusion to more explicitly immanent issues, she also, in leaving her post as editor of *The Dial*, challenged Emerson to assume a role fraught with just the sort of problems that compromise, or worse, consume writers (Richardson, 241).

In March 1842, Emerson became editor of *The Dial*, in what would be the halfway point of its existence. Begun in 1840, this journal aspired to be the clearinghouse for the best possible prose, regardless of authorial reputation or conceptual risk. Especially with Emerson at the helm, the magazine diversified its roster of contributors, which included, among many others, Thoreau, Fuller, and Hawthorne. Emerson published a great deal of his own work in this forum, from essays to poetry to literary criticism. But apparent self-publishing was as much to stimulate minds as sales. And the list of lesser-known writers far outnumbers the familiar ones. The intentions behind the production of the journal bear this out. In the first issue, the editors wrote:

> Our plan embraces much more than criticism; were it not so, our criticism would be naught. Everything noble is directed on life, and this is. We do not wish to say pretty or curious things, or to reiterate a few propositions in varied forms, but, if we can, to give expression to that spirit which lifts men to a higher platform, restores to them the religious sentiment, brings them worthy aims and pure pleasures, purges the inward eye, makes life less desultory, and, through raising man to the level of nature, takes away its melancholy from the landscape, and reconciles the practical with the speculative powers. . . .
> Our means correspond with the ends we have indicated. As

we wish not to multiply books, but to report life, our resources are therefore not so much the pens of practised writers, as the discourse of the living, and the portfolios which friendship has opened to us (*EP*, 332-3).

Though *The Dial* was short-lived (about four years), and Emerson's editorship was even shorter, the forum that it provided was significant for several reasons. Fuller and Emerson recognized the pool of talent and insight that surrounded them, and to which they contributed. They admitted the primary assumptions that drove them into their respective roles, namely, that their selection criteria were pointed to writing that turns us back to life, that makes us aware of and vulnerable to the world. The journal was used as a mechanism for harnessing these forces that orient us to the everyday, and for gathering them in such a way that their collective presentation might come to greater effect in reaching an audience. But even with a legitimated site of presentation, it is the editor that must shape and guide the content presented therein. In this respect, Emerson's contribution to *The Dial* at once shows his capacity for discerning and selecting work worth considering, and his continuing effort to reconceive the roles of his intellectual life.

For the duration of his writing life, Emerson was, in large measure, his own editor. This gives his work—whether an essay, a lecture, or a journal entry—a personal urgency since the words before us were placed by him (even if, in part, influenced by others). He read the final proofs, and signed off on them. While his tenure at *The Dial* came to an end, his work as an editor of his own work continued, as did many occasions of editing the work of others, including that of family members such as his aunt Mary Moody Emerson and his brother Charles, and that of friends such as Amos Bronson Alcott [1799-1888], Jones Very [1813-1880], Thoreau, and Carlyle. Even though Emerson had written so much, whether in his journals or in this journal, editing was not considered an onerous chore: it was itself a form of writing. This can be seen in Emerson's exhaustive indices to his journals (and indices to indices): in these volumes he created a system for managing what he had written so that he could draw upon it more efficiently when he wished to compose something more distended or continuous. It was by virtue of his editing skill that journal fragments written over the course of many years could be used to more pronounced effect in producing a single lecture or a series of essays.

4

Essays, America, and the Public Pulpit

In 1841, Emerson published his first collection of essays, entitled: *Essays*. When a second collection of essays was printed in 1844 and named *Essays: Second Series*, the first work was renamed—*Essays: First Series*. This may be a mundane fact about two mundane titles, but we should be able and allowed to see that these titles bend in homage to one of Emerson's privileged writers, Montaigne—someone who himself wrote two books of essays. But this is only to say that Emerson did not invent the genre in which he wrote. And he made no pretensions to believing that he had, since his reading was over-stuffed with this genre—from Seneca and Cicero to Montaigne and Bacon. Plutarch's moral writings are presupposed as an indelible influence. Emerson's two books of essays, thus, are best regarded as the heirs to the tradition of the moral essay, one that has long been suppressed or ignored by the intellectual habits of philosophers and scientists alike. These works are not just writings, they are *written*. In this way, the moral notions of Seneca seem literary and the scientific ideas of Bacon seem philosophical. Emerson's *Essays*—from both series—register distinctly in this line of pedigree, leaving the burden of classification to those who esteem it. Meanwhile, the rest can turn to Emerson's compass, to that space in which he draws from whatever field of life that suits him (science, history, literature, anthropology, poetry, biography, cultural criticism, philosophy, and others). Nothing seems off limits, nothing feels irrelevant.

Essays: First Series contains twelve essays: History, Self-Reliance, Compensation, Spiritual Laws, Love, Friendship, Prudence,

Heroism, The Over-Soul, Circles, Intellect, Art. *Essays: Second Series* contains eight essays: The Poet, Experience, Character, Manners, Gifts, Nature, Politics, Nominalist and Realist. And one lecture: "New England Reformers." Each essay, in both books, begins with an epigraph poem written by Emerson.

Half a year before the first book of essays was to appear, Emerson admitted to his journal: "I have been writing with some pains Essays on various matters as a sort of apology to my country for my apparent idleness" (October 7, 1840. *EJ*, 246). Emerson's "apology" is neither to say he is sorry for something he did, nor to write an *apologia* (that is, a defense of his ideas) for something he failed to do. Emerson's apology is an act of creation, an effort to counteract self-doubt and reinforce self-possession. In other words, Emerson's act of writing is a miniature version of America's apology in the middle years of the nineteenth century. In "The American Scholar," a few years earlier, Emerson hypothesized that America had not yet expressed itself as *America* since its students and citizens were, at once, far too deferential to Europe, and far "too busy to give to letters" (*EL*, 53). In his first breath before the Phi Beta Kappa Society, he said that "Our anniversary is one of hope, and, perhaps, not enough of labor" (*Ibid.*). Emerson "writing with some pains" is laboring, is in labor. From our vantage, we can see that Emerson was birthing himself, and to a significant degree birthing America (its letters, its thinking).

A few months after *Essays* was printed, Emerson was still at pains to explain his "apology for idleness." In his journal, he wrote:

> Thus how much of my reading & all my labor in house or garden seems mere waiting: any other could do it as well or better. It really seems to me of no importance—so little skill enters into these works, so little do they mix with my universal life—what I do, whether I hoe, or turn a grindstone, or copy manuscript, or eat my dinner. All my virtue consists in my consent to be insignificant which consent is founded on my faith in the great Optimism, which will justify itself to me at last (July, 1841. *EJ*, 255).

Emerson is masterful in his self-deprecation, but, to his benefit, he is equally as equipped to gather himself for recovery. If first we find him preparing to accede to his insignificance, we soon after find him founding his faith in a source of significance. This dialectic—this push and pull, this inhalation and exhalation—characterized Emerson's labor: his process of creating (for himself, and for America). The young American heard as much in "The American Scholar," when

Emerson said of *Man Thinking*: "In silence, in steadiness, in severe abstraction, let him hold by himself; add observation to observation, patient of neglect, patient of reproach; and bide his own time" (*EL*, 64). We must be reminded that creation requires a term of incubation, a period of internal development. As Emerson ends his essay "Experience," the sentiment of biding time is reiterated: "Patience and patience, we shall win at the last" (*EL*, 492). The burden for Emerson, for America, is to distinguish those labors that seem idle from those that merely require patience. It is the illusoriness of our self-perception that makes this a difficult burden: "In times when we thought ourselves indolent, we have afterwards discovered, that much was accomplished, and much was begun in us" (*EL*, 471). Afterwards, after words, consolation arrives. What was begun in us will, at last, emerge: "the inmost in due time becomes the outmost" (*EL*, 259).

Self-Reliance

Emerson is widely quoted, but perhaps no essay has been drawn from more than "Self-Reliance." This can be taken both as an indication of its content and of its influence. Its importance, much less its popularity, cannot be explained by saying that it is more accessible than other essays, or less enigmatic than other remarks. The attraction, it seems, lies squarely with the subject considered. Emerson's brief, but masterfully concentrated, essay depicts several formidable conflicts that confront the individual self in its relation to society, and by extension, that face a nation in search of its connection to history and the present world. "Self-Reliance" is folded upon itself so that it brings into relief questions that haunt the individual self as much as the self of America.

Positioned as if continuing Plato's discussion of the one and the many, Emerson frames the problem of conformity around the (im)possibility of harmonizing disparate parts, yet remaining able to distinguish them. How, for example, can an individual establish his or her own rules for life in an exercise of democratic principles, such as liberty (in speech and act), and at the same time bear inclusion in a group that defines rules for life in an exercise of imposition upon its members? In other words, in what way can I *belong* to myself and to a group without compromising my most cherished principles or uncritically adopting those recommended to me by others? How, for example, can I ever claim that I have produced something original (of and from myself), when every word I utter is part of an historical inheritance? Negotiating these questions, which have as much to do with originality and freedom as they do with imitation and constraint, becomes the driving project of the essay.

And that project begins with a claim that each individual possesses something worth both protecting and making vulnerable. Call the former a desire to remain whole, to be oneself; call the latter the recognition that risks of expression must be taken in order to achieve and secure self-identity (however precarious or provisional). In the essay, this two-stroke phenomenon is referred to as "genius," "Instinct," and "the aboriginal Self," but the common referent is the individual and his or her ownmost thoughts. Too often, however, one fails to safeguard himself or herself against the penetrating influences of others, and therefore, one fails to make known to others how such influences obscure one's capacity for *self*-definition and *self*-expression. Emerson does not deny that one benefits from the environment in which one lives, but that, on occasion, that environment (made up of all sorts of people, things, ideas, and institutions) can make it easy for one to neglect what seems most essentially one's own.

> To believe your own thought, to believe that what is true for you in your private heart is true for all men,—that is genius. Speak your latent conviction, and it shall be the universal sense; for the inmost in due time becomes the outmost. . . . Familiar as the voice of the mind is to each, the highest merit we ascribe to Moses, Plato, and Milton is, that they set at naught books and traditions, and spoke not what men but what they thought. A man should learn to detect and watch that gleam of light which flashes across his mind from within, more than the luster of the firmament of bards and sages. Yet he dismisses without notice his thought, because it is his. In every work of genius we recognize our own rejected thoughts: they come back to us with a certain alienated majesty (*EL*, 259).

Just because one feels that a private thought is "true," does not make it so. The truth here referenced in neither one of objectivity, nor of consensus: it is of expression. The reason Emerson admires Moses, Plato, and Milton is his feeling that they did not mimic inherited ideas, but attempted to secure their own thoughts in what was said or done. (And his choice of figures is not inconsequential: a prophet, a philosopher, and a poet. These are names for permutations of possibility in our own ways of being in the world.) This can be read as a development of Emerson's earlier bid that we seek an "original relation" to the world (*EL*, 7). One is not to be preoccupied with being right, but instead with cultivating a talent for honesty. The assumption that greatness—no matter its kind—is the exclusive domain of others, is the assumption to discard. Emerson continues from above:

> . . . Great works of art have no more affecting lesson for us than this. They teach us to abide by our spontaneous impression with good-humored inflexibility then most when the whole cry of voices is on the other side. Else, to-morrow a stranger will say with masterly good sense precisely what we have thought and felt all the time, and we shall be forced to take with shame our own opinion from another (*EL*, 259).

Emerson replaces Socrates' primary creed—Know Thyself—with the more necessary: "Trust thyself" (*EL*, 260). We are brought to see that knowledge is deprived of its value when held by him or her lacking self-trust. Such knowledge is merely academic, since it serves only to relate bits of knowledge to other bits of knowledge, but never quite to life, or the practice of living. The threats to one's "good-humored inflexibility" are many, widespread, and unceasing. But Emerson imagines that there is a method for mediating such threats, and even thriving in spite of them:

> These are the voices which we hear in solitude, but they grow faint and inaudible as we enter into the world. Society everywhere is in a conspiracy against the manhood of every one of its members. Society is a joint-stock company, in which the members agree, for the better securing of his bread to each shareholder, to surrender the liberty and culture of the eater. The virtue in most request is conformity. Self-reliance is its aversion. It loves not realities and creators, but names and customs (*EL*, 261).

Emerson denies that our social economy does best by means of the compromised liberties and imaginations of its members. The homogeneity of a given product makes it easier to handle, sort, and stock. This may be a hallmark benefit of dealing with things, but it cannot be when dealing with persons. Hence, it is much harder for society to cope with difference(s). Because of this, its members suffer the anxiety of finding a way to "fit in." The problem is not how I can be like others, but how I can be (like) myself and not be considered "other." Emerson envisions three scenarios, only the last of which he deems worth pursuing:

> What I must do is all that concerns me, not what the people

think. This rule, equally arduous in actual and in intellectual life, may serve for the whole distinction between greatness and meanness. It is the harder, because you will always find those who think they know what is your duty better than you know it. It is easy in the world to live after the world's opinion; it is easy in solitude to live after your own; but the great man is he who in the midst of the crowd keeps with perfect sweetness the independence of solitude (*EL*, 263).

If one decides to remain true to one's principles, we may regard that faith as virtuous. But such steadfastness, it is shown, cinches one's capacity for growth; the possibility of change (even in subtle nuance) is diminished. The serene and confident advocate of one's beliefs may soon find that he or she is no longer a seeker or an experimenter, but a dogmatist. Retracting from the spirit of science, one finds solace not in testing, but in proclaiming. In an effort to stabilize life, one slowly begins to destroy its potential for enhancement. Aware of this, and cautious of its consequences, Emerson rallies behind the idea that there is a fair measure more virtue in *inconsistency* than conventionally supposed. Being inconsistent does not mean sometimes being late to an appointment, or failing to always apply certain rules of grammar when writing. It means remaining poised for alteration in belief and in conduct.

The other terror that scares us from self-trust is our consistency; a reverence for our past act or word, because the eyes of others have no other data for computing our orbit than our past acts, and we are loathe to disappoint them.

But why should you keep your head over your shoulder? Why drag about this corpse of your memory, lest you contradict somewhat you have stated in this or that public place? Suppose you should contradict yourself; what then?

. . . A foolish consistency is the hobgoblin of little minds, adored by little statesmen and philosophers and divines. With consistency a great soul has simply nothing to do. He may as well concern himself with his shadow on the wall. Speak what you think now in hard words, and to-morrow speak what to-morrow thinks in hard words again, though it contradict every thing you said to-day (*EL*, 265).

Emerson is not calling for anarchy, or for us to adopt some antinomian worldview. The admonition does not concern consistency so much as consistency misused—what he types "foolish." Holding fast to some view because the view was held before, even though you no longer agree with it, can be considered "foolish consistency." Though the gesture here is meant to liberate us from false pretenses, it also complicates just how we might go about defining what is and what is not a misuse of consistency. How will I know when I am being foolishly consistent? Emerson's criterion for such knowledge is to overcome one's preoccupation with the habit of being consistent (another way of saying faithful). Contradicting what you thought, therefore, shows that there is movement in your thinking—not that thinking has come to an end.

The Hyacinth Boy

On January 24, 1842, ten months after *Essays: First Series* was published, Emerson's five-year old son, Waldo, became ill with scarlatina. As with any ailment facing a child, one expects that the young body will sustain the trauma and fully recover. But within a few days, Waldo developed a severe fever. By the evening of the twenty-seventh he was dead.

The quick on-set of the disease, coupled with its rapid and fatal outcome, overwhelmed Emerson, his family, and his closest circle of friends. Within a day of Waldo's death, Emerson wrote nearly a dozen letters, each charged of equal measures grief and guilt, and lined with a thin beam of acquiescence. He sent word to Mary Moody Emerson and Margaret Fuller, to Elizabeth Palmer Peabody and Elizabeth Hoar that "the most severe of all afflictions has befallen me, in the death of my boy" (January 28, 1842. *L*, vol. III, 8). A month later, he wrote to Thomas Carlyle of a future imagination now erased: "How often I have pleased myself that one day I should send to you, this Morningstar of mine, & stay at home so gladly behind such a representative!" (February 28, 1842. *EC*, 317). To Caroline Sturgis, he wrote something that would soon after be adapted for his essay "Experience:"

> Alas! I chiefly grieve that I cannot grieve; that this fact takes no more deep hold than other facts, is as dreamlike as they; a lambent flame that will not burn playing on the surface of my river. Must every experience—those that promised to be dearest & most penetrative,—only kiss my cheek like the wind & pass away? (February 4, 1842. *L*, vol. VII, 485).

And in his journals, Emerson committed a long entry of remembrance, including these lines:

> Sorrow makes us all children again, destroys all differences of
> intellect. The wisest knows nothing.
> It seems as if I ought to call upon the winds to describe my
> boy, my fast receding boy, a child of so large & generous a nature
> that I cannot paint him by specialties, as I might another (January
> 30, 1842. *EJ*, 277).

The boy did not, it turns out, recede at all fast from Emerson's memory.
Twenty years later, he wrote of Waldo with direct quotation, and
immediate emotion:

> Little Waldo, when I carried him to the circus, & showed him
> the clown & his antics, said, "It makes me want to go home," and I
> am forced to quote my boy's speech often & often since. I can do
> so few things, I can see so few companies, that do not remind me
> of it! Of course, if I had the faculty to meet the occasion, I should
> enjoy it. Not having it, & noting how many occasions I cannot
> meet, life loses value every month, & I shall be quite ready to give
> place to whoso waits for my chair (August 26, 1862. *EJ*, 503-4).

The most formidable distillate of Emerson's grief, however, can be
found in his long, loving poetic elegy to his lost son, "Threnody."
Here, a father's grief is let loose in language. Emerson writes both in
celebration of the wonderful joys his son brought, and of the unreal
reality that his absence has left.

> Now Love and Pride, alas! In vain,
> Up and down their glances strain.
> The painted sled stands where it stood;
> The kennel by the corded wood;
> The gathered sticks to stanch the wall
> Of the snow-tower, when snow should fall;
> The ominous hole he dug in the sand,
> And childhood's castles built of planned;
> His daily haunts I well discern,—
> The poultry-yard, the shed, the barn,—
> And every inch of garden ground
> Paced by the blessed feet around,
> From the roadside to the brook
> Whereinto he loved to look.

Step the meek birds where erst they ranged;
The wintry garden lies unchanged;
The brook into the stream runs on;
But the deep-eyed boy is gone (*CP*, 119).

Now Waldo's hole dug in the sand, seems a prescient grave. Looking out to the everyday tools and toys, with which his son played, Emerson still sees him there engaged. Those boyish haunts now haunt the father. The presence of Waldo's absence proved ineluctable. And so the last words Emerson spoke in his life must haunt us: "Oh, that beautiful boy" (McLeer, 27).

Experience

As any father would be who has lost his son, Emerson was understandably distraught. The deaths of loved ones had punctuated his life, since his father died when he was seven. He endured the deaths of his youngest and most beloved brother Charles, his first wife Ellen, and his brother Edward—all taken prematurely. And, in years to come, he would suffer the tragic losses of profound and dear friends, including Thoreau (taken by tuberculosis) and Fuller (drowned at sea). In the years and months leading up to the publication of Emerson's second collection of essays, it was Waldo's death that seemed to weigh heaviest upon him.

To a significant degree, "Experience," the second essay of the *Essays: Second Series*, is a meditation on disorientation. Experiencing the death of others may easily catalyze such a state, descending upon one as if a private cloud. One may seek first to ascertain where one is, and only afterwards, how to go on from there. The essay begins, therefore, with a question of how orientation can be re-established.

Where do we find ourselves? In a series of which we do not know the extremes, and believe that it has none? (*EL*, 471)

The cause of this lostness, of this search to be found, is doubt. Emerson is no longer sure about his place, and the placement of things that surround him. But he has come to believe in one thing—in his skepticism. And it is through questioning his doubts about the world that he works to find a way through it.

Sleep lingers all our lifetime about our eyes, as night hovers all day in the boughs of the fir-tree. All things swim and glitter. Our life

59

is not so much threatened as our perception. Ghostlike we glide through nature, and should not know our place again (*EL*, 471).

Like unsettled spirits of the afterworld, it seems, we are no better able to navigate our way through the world, no more adept at finding our proper place and proper work, than these ephemerals of the imagination. We haunt the world because, Emerson conjectures, our ability to perceive it is compromised. We do not see the world as it is, but as a sort of phantasm or semblance.

Dream delivers us to dream, and there is no end to illusion. Life is a train of moods like a string of beads, and, as we pass through them, they prove to be many-colored lenses which paint the world their own hue, and each shows only what lies in its focus (*EL*, 473).

Life itself is a bubble and a skepticism, and a sleep within a sleep. Grant it, and as much more as they will,—but thou, God's darling! heed thy private dream: thou wilt not be missed in the scorning and skepticism. . . (*EL*, 481).

We have learned that we do no see directly, but mediately, and that we have no means of correcting these colored and distorting lenses which we are, or of computing the amount of their errors (*EL*, 487).

But are these not words spoken in the shock of witnessing death? At such times, does the world not cease to have order, and do we not feel at once displaced from our former position? The death of others is so incomprehensible, so painful, that in order to cope with it, we enter a state of disbelief. Grief inspires us to question the character of reality, and in so doing, unsettles the habits of belief we have been accustomed to. There is a temptation, at such times, which makes us wonder whether we can learn something from the experience—as if to be compensated for our losses. It is because we are unable to receive this lesson that we feel justified in thinking our grief is not fleeting, but permanent.

People grieve and bemoan themselves, but it is not half so bad with them as they say. There are moods in which we court suffering, in the hope that here, at least, we shall find reality, sharp peaks and edges of truth. But it turns out to be scene-painting and

60

counterfeit. The only thing grief has taught me, is to know how shallow it is. That, like all the rest, plays about the surface, and never introduces me into the reality, for contact with which, we would even pay the costly price of sons and lovers (*EL*, 472-3).

Emerson has already paid this price. And he received neither instruction, nor contact for his tuition. When we are sure that nothing could hurt us more than we have already been hurt, we become numb to the world. In the interstitial space between my pain and the world, there seems an unbreachable distance. Emerson begins to suspect that grieving merely highlights this condition in us. Human perception is not just impaired when we encounter the rare and exceptional events of life—the traumas of lost "sons and lovers"—but in everyday experiences.

Was it Boscovich who found that bodies never come in contact? Well, souls never touch their objects. An innavigable sea washes with silent waves between us and the things we aim at and converse with. Grief too will make us idealists (*EL*, 473).

I grieve that grief can teach me nothing, nor carry me one step into real nature (*Ibid.*).

In the wake of disaster, we crave endlessly and, it seems, hopelessly for something to fill the space of loss. Despite losing his son, and so many dear others, Emerson reckons that there might be some benefit in the experiences *if only* he could feel *touched* by them. But he cannot. This is what grief has taught him. No matter how desperate things become, I will not be able to feel, to think, to remember, to make contact with them as I need to.

But Emerson *has* learned something, namely, that moods are not emotional states, but existential conditions. His metaphor for this is "subject-lenses" (*EL*, 487). Our perception of the world is forever mediated by some interfering membrane that blurs, or colors, or otherwise distorts a full and true experience.

[W]e cannot say too little of our constitutional necessity of seeing things under private aspects, or saturated with our humors. . . . We must hold hard to this poverty, however scandalous, and by more vigorous self-recoveries, after the sallies of action, possess our axis more firmly (*EL*, 490).

When Emerson asks "Where do we find ourselves?" he can be seen as inquiring after the character of the *present* location ("Where is it that we find ourselves *right now*?"), and asking about a different, *absent* location ("Since this is not the place, where *do* we find ourselves?). Take his notion of "constitutional necessity" as a reply to both variations of this question. It is another way of saying, we are limited, or more familiarly, we are fated.

Emerson briefly adduces the forces that seem to shape our lives:

> Illusion, Temperament, Succession, Surface, Surprise, Reality, Subjectiveness,—these are the threads on the loom of time, these are the lords of life (*EL*, 491).

Pulling together some of Emerson's metaphors here, we can see that "life is a flux of moods," and that moods are "like a string of beads," which prove to be "many-colored lenses" (*EL*, 485, 473). Imagining these mood-beads hanging on the several "threads" that comprise "the lords of life," an image of fate emerges. Our "constitutional necessity" is one in which we are ever entwined with some incapacity (viz., Illusion, Temperament, Succession, et al.), and at the same time find our perception of the world mediated by some influence (i.e., some mood).

We find ourselves, then, inscribed by a condition that seems at once fatal and common.

> We thrive by casualties. Our chief experiences have been casual (*EL*, 483).

So it is that the most perilous aspects of our lives (casualties) are also the least particular and most plentiful (casual). Our fate is bearable because it is shared, a part of everyday life. Instead of seeing life as made of a few exceptionally important and despairingly difficult days (days with casualties), Emerson is trying to show us how *every* day is weighted similarly, or at least, with similar potential.

> Suffice it for the joy of the universe, that we have not arrived at a wall, but at interminable oceans. Our life seems not present, so much as prospective; not for the affairs on which it is wasted, but as a hint of this vast-flowing vigor (*EL*, 486).

If "the lords of life" made it seem that the fated circumstances of human life are bleak because unflatteringly limited, then the idea that in the ordinary experiences of life we face "interminable oceans" should correct for a desperate picture. But even oceans have their shores, and their floors. Yet, how much remains in the spaces *between* these limits?

If we will take the good we find, asking no questions, we shall have heaping measures. The great gifts are not got by analysis. Everything good is on the highway. The middle region of our being is the temperate zone. We may climb into the thin and cold realm of pure geometry and lifeless science, or sink into that of sensation. Between these extremes is the equator of life, of thought, of spirit, of poetry,—a narrow belt. Moreover, in popular experience, everything good is on the highway (*EL*, 480).

The imagery is piling up somewhat. And yet, the primary concern remains uncluttered. We are constrained both by a myriad of forces (internal and external), and still, within the bounds of that constraint—as it were, on the highway of life—we find that there is much that can be done. Individual power, therefore, resides in that region where power can be exercised.

Onward and onward! In liberated moments, we know that a new picture of life and duty is already possible; the elements already exist in many minds around you, of a doctrine of life which shall transcend any written record we have. The new statement will comprise the skepticisms, as well as the faiths of society, and out of unbeliefs a creed shall be formed. For, skepticisms are not gratuitous or lawless, but are limitations of the affirmative statement, and the new philosophy must take them in, and make affirmations outside of them, just as much as it must include the oldest beliefs (*EL*, 486-7).

This parable could be taken as describing the very essay in which it is included. How much does "Experience" become evidence of just this sort of conversion? That is, of drawing on "casualties" and the "casual" with an eye to showing their synonymy? The same can be said for the relation between skepticism and faith, between doubt and belief. Emerson's "Experience" is a "new statement" of Emerson's experience. And that experience is defined by its recognition of life's limits as much as its powers of possibility. It should, then, not be unsettling to discover how intimately Emerson links antagonistic forces. It is by sight of their apposition that we stand on the verge of

63

finding a way to respond to our condition (whether we are lost, or just trying to get clearer about where we are).

> Patience and patience, we shall win at the last. We must be very suspicious of the deceptions of the element of time. It takes a good deal of time to eat or to sleep, or to earn a hundred dollars, and a very little time to entertain a hope and an insight which becomes the light of our life. . . . Never mind the ridicule, never mind the defeat: up again, old heart!—it seems to say,—there is victory yet for all justice; and the true romance which the world exists to realize, will be the transformation of genius into practical power (*EL*, 492).

With this said, with a sort of response to skepticism made, it is still quite difficult not to take Emerson's words about losing his son as ironical. One wonders if his hyperbole in one direction (i.e., toward numbness) is not meant to represent an exaggeration in the other (i.e., toward extreme sensitivity). Emerson was so touched by his son's death that he feels untouchable. His grief is so acute that the exceptional pain becomes familiar. And for this he feels a survivor's guilt, which he interprets as a sufficient reason for calling metaphysics into question—as if this were the only way he could survive such loss, and at last regain orientation. How much must one bear to get back one's bearing?

> In the death of my son, now more than two years ago, I seem to have lost a beautiful estate,—no more. I cannot get it nearer to me. If tomorrow I should be informed of the bankruptcy of my principle debtors, the loss of my property would be a great inconvenience to me, perhaps, for many years; but it would leave me as it found me,—neither better nor worse. So it is with this calamity: it does not touch me: some thing which I fancied was a part of me, which could not be torn away without tearing me, nor enlarged without enriching me, falls off from me, and leaves no scar. It was caducous (*EL*, 473).

At first glance, these might be taken as insensitive remarks, as something someone would say who could *not feel*. But Emerson reports that he has been devastated by having been left untouched, and by this he means that he has been denied his chance to mourn. He is asking us: What have *I* lost? If it is the calamity I believe it is, why am I alright? We are then left to ask ourselves: How does one *show* one's grief? Emerson would be glad to have a mark that made clear what the loss of his son meant, for then he could explain both his loss, and his lostness. With such a sign, Emerson might be able to find his way about, and by reference to it—go on.

Steam, Simulation, and the Traversals of Technology

The technological innovations that span Emerson's life, and therefore most of the nineteenth century, in some cases, radically reconfigured the possibilities of human experience. In 1833, after a seemingly interminable six-week voyage from Boston Harbor to Malta, Emerson sped across the Mediterranean from Sicily to Naples in a steamship—his first experience on such a fast moving vessel. The impact of the steamship would become even more pronounced when returning home from his second trip to Europe, in 1848, he made the trans-Atlantic passage in just twelve days. The distance between continents had not changed, and yet Boston seemed closer to London.

> Yet in hurrying over these abysses, whatever dangers we are running into, we are certainly running out of the risks of hundreds of miles every day, which have their own chances of squall, collision, sea-stroke, piracy, cold and thunder. Hour for hour, the risk on a steam-boat is great; but the speed is safety, or twelve days of danger instead of twenty-four (*CW*, vol. V, 27).

Emerson's calculus about the comparative risks and advantages of the steamship are matched by his intrigue over the fecundity of steam. With a sense for the magnitude of production made possible by steam-driven machines, he writes, in *English Traits*:

> The power of machinery in Great Britain, in mills, has been computed to be equal to 600,000,000 men, one man being able by the aid of steam to do the work which required two hundred and fifty men to accomplish fifty years ago (*CW*, vol. V, 159).

Emerson's astonishment is hardly unjustified, and the implication of the promise therein posed seems likewise equally understandable. Harnessed steam—whether in the ship or on the rail, so it was shown, not only changed the human relationship to labor, but also to space and time. As Emerson once told of his friend: "Mr. Thoreau explained to the President [of Harvard College] that the railroad had destroyed the old scale of distances" (*EP*, 401). And Emerson, in "The Fugitive

Slave Law" address, which he delivered to the people of Concord in 1851, spoke cautiously of our uses of and excuses for new technologies: "I cannot accept the railroad and telegraph in exchange for reason and charity. It is not skill in iron locomotives that makes so fine civility, as the jealousy of liberty. I cannot think the most judicious tubing a compensation for metaphysical debility" (*CW*, vol. XI, 183). Here the political and ethical consequences of technology come to light so that we do not just speak of the liberation of labor, and the modulation of time and space, but the emancipation of human beings. Steam might propel the engine of freedom, but it will not grant us the resources for securing it. The latter is not a technological issue. "Many facts concur to show that we must look deeper for our salvation than to steam, photographs, balloons or astronomy" (*CW*, vol. VII, 164).

The daguerreotype, an early photographic process, was coming in to prominence at mid-century, and Emerson had several portraits taken of himself and his family (including one of his son, Waldo, just a few months before he died). It was at this point a rarefied and expensive process, perhaps at first not quite able to overcome its sense of novelty. Emerson slowly filled his home with photographs, having them line the walls and stairwell. In 1870's *Society and Solitude*, Emerson gives a sign that the novelty was wearing off, and that the photograph, and other coincident technologies, did indeed yield a privilege: ". . . we pity our fathers for dying before steam and galvanism, photograph and spectroscope arrived, as cheated out of half their human estate" (*CW*, vol. VII, 158).

But it was the railroad that proved the most influential on the contour of Emerson's experience as it became the principle means that enabled his career as a mobile lecturer. The train car, as an enclosed, fast-moving projectile, made the windows into screens. Each window framed a new image, or became a frame in a sequence of images (a proto-cinematic experience). The passing landscape was like so many moving pictures. The habits of Emerson's mid-nineteenth century perception make travel seem a form of hallucination. In 1843, Emerson remarked in his journal:

> Dreamlike travelling on the railroad. The towns through which I pass between Phila.[delphia] & New York, make no distinct impression. They are like pictures on a wall. The more, that you can read all the way in the car a French novel (February 7, 1843. *EJ*, 300).

In "Experience," the following year, he writes, as if in translation of his time on the railroad, about the transitoriness of experience—"in the necessity of a succession of moods or objects" (*EL*, 476). Though we desire permanence, it is not suited to us. Though we should like to dwell in one place, we must move on. He continues:

> So with pictures; each will bear an emphasis of attention once, which it cannot retain, though we fain would continue to be pleased in that manner. How strongly I have felt of pictures, that when you have seen one well, you must take your leave of it; you shall never see it again (*Ibid.*).

Whether the "pictures" are daguerreotypes or the view out of the framed railcar windows, or even the books and persons we have grown used to concentrating upon, we cannot become complacent in our view. "When, at night, I look at the moon and stars, I seem stationary, and they to hurry. Our love of the real draws us to permanence, but health of body consists in circulation, and sanity of mind in variety or facility of association (*Ibid.*).

As early as 1836 (in *Nature*), Emerson was sensitive to the intimate relationship between photographic impressions, and those made possible by the locomotive. The movement of the train alters the perception of objects in a way comparable to the camera's capture and focus of light.

> What new thoughts are suggested by seeing a face of country quite familiar, in the rapid movement of the railroad car! Nay, the most wonted objects, (make a very slight change in the point of vision), please us most. In a camera obscura, the butcher's cart, and the figure of one of our own family gratifies us. Turn the eyes upside down, by looking at the landscape through your legs, and how agreeable is the picture, though you have seen it any time these twenty years! (*CW*, vol. I, 51).

The *camera obscura* always projects an inverted image. By bending down, and peeking through our legs, we, in effect, mimic that manner of reversed imaging. The body becomes a camera, now able to see the world in a novel way—as if for the first time. (How might we re-read Emerson's image of the "transparent eye-ball" with this in mind?)

The railroad, like the steamship and photograph, and later in Emerson's life—the telegraph, are recognized for their affect upon human subjective experience and materially objective conditions. As he noted in the 1840's about the influence of steam on manufacturing, in the 1870's, Emerson bears report to the contribution made by emerging technologies on the vast American land and the country's growing population:

> Here in America are all the wealth of soil, of timber, of mines and of the sea, put into the possession of a people who wield all these wonderful machines, have the secret of steam, of electricity; and have the power and habit of invention in their brain. We Americans have got suppled into the state of melioration. Life is always rapid here, but what acceleration to its pulse in ten years,—what in the four years of the war! We have seen the railroad and telegraph subdue our enormous geography. . . (*CW*, vol. VIII, 141).

The motif of movement remains in steady use because it so aptly describes the energy of the people spurred by the energies being employed. Even in his admiration of these new feats of invention and engineering, Emerson puns the dynamism that pervades the terrain and its inhabitants: "Our eyes run approvingly along the lengthened lines of railroad and telegraph" (*CW*, vol. VII, 283).

Emerson's lecturing itinerary, from the early 1830's to 1860's, reflects the growing prevalence of the railroad. The more lines of rail laid, and the further away they were put down, meant the more he could travel, the further away he could go. At the outset of his career, Emerson gave few lectures, and when he did, they were not far from home. By the mid-1840's, with a growing reputation and an expanding rail system, he was giving more lectures (about four or five dozen each year) and across a wider geographical area—not just in Boston, but in Providence, New York, and Philadelphia (Richardson, 418). In the 1850's, his circuit swelled to include nearly eighty speaking engagements per year. And his routes elongated as well: he spoke in St. Louis and Minneapolis, and traveled as far as California. In four decades of lecturing, Emerson made almost fifteen hundred presentations. In his most active twenty-five years, this work took him away from home as much as half the year, every year (*Ibid.*).

The increasing number of lectures, and the enhanced geographic scope of his audience, however, misses, alas, the grueling pace at which he traveled. This rapid rate—for the running eye—is made possible solely by the expanse and efficiency of the railroad. To get a sense for the exhausting rhythm of his travels, consider this report of a brief itinerary:

On a typical trip he either lectured or traveled by train to the next town almost every day for months on end. One two-week stretch in the winter of 1855 had him in Rochester, New York, on February 15, in Syracuse on the sixteenth, Rome on the seventeenth, Oneida on the nineteenth, Vernon on the twentieth. Then he went back to Rochester on the twenty-first, to Lockport on the twenty-second, Hamilton, Ontario, on the twenty-third, back to Syracuse on the twenty-fourth, to Canandaigua on the twenty-sixth, Watertown on the twenty-eighth, and Cazenovia on the first of March. That makes 12 speaking engagements in two weeks, each one involving a train trip (Richardson, 419).

Emerson was one of those American's inventing new relationships to people and places by means of technologies. Where once his constituency did not exceed a few square miles of quiet, metropolitan Boston, it now stretched from New York Harbor to San Francisco Bay. Steam propelled the locomotive on new tracks. And from his railcar seat Emerson could see, with his rapidly moving camera-eye, "this new, yet approachable America," framed in a dizzying horizontal blur—the motion-picture, the movement of a man faced with a new world (*EL*, 485).

Representative Men

In one sense, to say that something is "representative" is to say that it is indicative of the class of things it stands for. Thus, a given Macintosh may be representative of apples. In this way, there is nothing remarkable about the specific apple: it merely gives a sense of a category of fruit. In a more nuanced sense, however, to say that something is "representative" is to say that it is rare, and not at all usual. This is the use of "representative" Emerson employs in the title of his work *Representative Men*, published in 1850. These figures do not give us a sense of the features that are most common among men, but the inverse. They are representative in being *a*typical instances. Thus, it can be somewhat misleading to call them "representative men" since Emerson does not select them because they represent man, but precisely because they *do not* represent man. To be even more precise: they represent themselves.

Each man is used as an anecdote, as an illustration of an exceptional moment in imagination, in thinking, in the application of will, in the power of belief, in the craft of artistry. Emerson's representative men are, indeed, unrepresentative. They are rare and exceptional. And that is why he heralds and herds them for our attention. The moral is not to be like them by doing what they did, but to be like them by doing what *we* do. It is in this way that we too may become representative—not the best instances of humankind, but the best instances of ourselves.

Emerson accused most human speech of being borrowed, that is, of being appropriated from the minds and voices of others. In "Self-Reliance," this is called "conformity," and it finds its natural antagonism with the performance of self-trust. We are to be weary of neglecting our own thoughts because they are our own. And yet, concomitantly, Emerson fathoms that we are neither to be incurious, nor naively dismissive of history. Thus, we are put into a paradox wherein we wish to learn from our predecessors and contemporaries, and at the same time must guard against letting those lessons arbitrate our own posterity. How can I steel myself to "shun father and mother and wife and brother, when my genius calls me" *and* acknowledge and appreciate the degree to which society makes my thoughts possible (*EL*, 262)? If history and culture presuppose my thoughts, in what sense can I say such thoughts are mine? It is in *Representative Men*, and especially its leading chapter—"Uses of Great Men"—that Emerson attends to this confounding conflict.

One would like to know how one becomes who one is. For the most part, it seems that we are the accumulations of several histories—at the least, anthropological and genetic. In "Self-Reliance," Emerson's appeal to the "aboriginal Self" makes it seem as if one emerged and matured *ex nihilo*, that is, without any external influences (*EL*, 268). So suspicious of the harming influence of others, Emerson can seem to recommend dislocation from society and disregard for others. In "Uses of Great Men," Emerson tempers his trepidation by signaling not just *who* we should use to reinforce ourselves, but *how* to use them. Principally, "[o]ther men are lenses through which we read our own minds" (*EL*, 616). And they "clear our eyes" so that we can "see other people and their works" (*EL*, 626). Seeing these exemplars is an excitation of our own imagination.

> When this wakes, a man seems to multiply ten times or a thousand times his force. It opens the delicious sense of indeterminate size, and inspires an audacious mental habit (*EL*, 622).

By, as it were, enacting the dictates of his or her genius, the exemplar inspires us to consider wider limits for the influence of personal power. Emerson had claimed that "our reading is mendicant and sycophantic," but this is reading that fails to register the provocation of texts (*EL*, 268). Reading is not supposed to humiliate, and reinforce one's sense of inadequacy; rather, it is to provide an indication of what is possible.

> We are elastic as the gas of gunpowder, and a sentence in a book, or a word dropped in conversation, sets free our fancy, and instantly our heads are bathed with galaxies... (*EL*, 622).

Still, we must guard against the tendency to over-celebrate the influence such humans and texts can have. "Our delight in reason degenerates into idolatry of the herald" (*EL*, 623). In the "excess of influence of the great man," we retreat from our work, our ideas (*EL*, 627). "His attractions warp us from our place. We have become underlings and intellectual suicides" (*Ibid.*). We might call this the *mis*use of great men, and its result is nothing short of "oppression."

> The imbecility of men is always inviting the impudence of power. It is the delight of vulgar talent to dazzle and to bind the beholder. But true genius seeks to defend us from itself. True genius will not impoverish, but will liberate, and add new senses... (*EL*, 623).

The representative, therefore, will not dispossess me of myself, but aid in the prospect and execution of that possession. Too often, Emerson worries, we dislocate ourselves from the community of greatness, either fearing that we cannot contribute, or that the burden of contribution is too high. "The cheapness of man is every day's tragedy. It is as real a loss that others should be low, as that we should be low, for we must have society" (*EL*, 629). That is, we must realize that living in society, in the low, is not incommensurable with achieving greatness. There are "no common men," but "men are at last of a size: and true art is possible, on the conviction that every talent has its apotheosis somewhere" (*EL*, 630). Emerson's representative men are hardly common. Their uncommonness, Emerson concludes, derives from the talent for achieving genius in the context of the everyday, in the midst of people, in the currents of the current age.

At first blush, it can seem that in writing of Plato, Swedenborg, Montaigne, Shakespeare, Napoleon, and Goethe, Emerson is attempting to configure a new pantheon, the quick purpose of which would be to posit a (new) scale against which to measure ourselves. These lectures, however, are meant to establish no such gauge. "No man, in all the procession of famous men, is reason or illumination, or that essence we were looking for; but is an exhibition, in some quarter, of new possibilities" (*EL*, 630). We cannot uncritically adopt the patterns or performances of their lives. Indulging in the effect of tautology, one could say: Goethe was Goethe. If we are to learn from Goethe, or the others, we cannot pursue a simple-minded imitation. Emerson told us that "imitation is suicide," the former setting the conditions for the dire consequences of the latter (*EL*, 259). Emerson, again and again, guards us from the habit of moving from "dignity to dependence," wherein the great man becomes our oppressor instead of our liberator. To this end, Emerson must apprise us of the difference between seeing a representative figure as a model for emulation, and (more modestly) as an instance of life lived in honor of its capacities and possibilities. In "Self-Reliance," Emerson works to reinforce this sense of relation: "When private men shall act with original views, the lustre will be transferred from the actions of kings to those of gentlemen" (*EL*, 268). Greatness is not a lost, foreign attribute, but a proximate, familiar potentiality:

> No greater men are now than ever were. . . . Phocion, Socrates, Anaxagoras, Diogenes, are great men, but they leave no class. He who is really of their class will not be called by their name, but will be his own man, and, in his turn, the founder of a sect (*EL*, 280).

It may be easy to mistake the sentiment of Emerson's book, *Representative Men*, and his essay "The Uses of Great Men," because these works, with their words "Great" and "Men," appear to offend modern sensibilities. Emerson can seem not only misogynistic, but elitist—anti-democratic. This is not the case, and most of the impression can be blamed on conventions of language. Emerson is, contrariwise, aiming to show that these "great men" are representative human beings because they abided by something we *all* have the potential to honor and promote (in his work, most commonly referred to as "genius"). That Emerson's book has so few figures is not a comment on what is to come, but on what has been.

English Traits

When Emerson was born, America was only twenty-seven years old. The official ties to England had been cut by a declaration of independence, but there remained—in the living memory of many

American citizens—the still palpable influence of that empire. By 1833, Emerson made his first voyage to England, and in 1847, he embarked on a second. As was his habit, Emerson kept a journal record of these trips. In 1856, drawing, in part, from his many notes, he compiled the book *English Traits*, which amounts to the fusion of autobiography, cultural history, and meditation on lineage. If America was England's progeny, either in fact or in symbol, it would be worth considering, in some measure, what its English traits might be. The book serves as a genetics of England according to Emerson, including the defining traits of the country and its inhabitants, and also a record of how Emerson formatted (or formalized) his own experiences and impressions of the same. Thus, the work, as Emerson's work tends to do, serves a private purpose even as it addresses a public interest (and often a public need).

Though America in Emerson's day was already a nation defined by its diversity of immigrants, England remained the solitary symbol of maternality. America, despite the presence of Chinese and Arab, Spaniard and African, maintained the habit of seeing England as the origin, if not of its culture entire, then of the standards and customs it wished to emulate. This was especially the case in Boston, where the provinciality of New England stood in awe of the grand worldliness of Old England. When Emerson wrote, England was a global empire, but America was (only) an empire in the making—indeed an empire that wished to grow without mimicking the imperial spirit. And yet, Emerson was born less than a month after Thomas Jefferson secured the $15 million dollar purchase of the Louisiana territory—indicative of a different style of conquest. America would expand in business terms—by mergers and acquisitions, and on occasion, takeovers. And, notoriously, by breaking certain contracts.

In a conversation with Thomas Carlyle, Emerson humbly confessed his attraction to England, yet also admitted his suspicion that America would by and by overshadow its parent:

> I told C.[arlyle] that I was easily dazzled, and was accustomed to concede readily all that an Englishman would ask; I saw everywhere in the country proofs of sense and spirit, and success of every sort: I like the people: they are as good as they are handsome; they have everything, and can do everything: but meantime, I surely know, that, as soon as I return to Massachusetts, I shall lapse at once into the feeling, which the geography of American inevitably inspires, that we play the game with immense advantage; that there and not here is the seat and

center of the British race; and that no skill or activity can long compete with the prodigious natural advantages of that country, in the hands of the same race; and that England, an old and exhausted island, must one day be contented, like other parents, to be strong only in her children. But this was a proposition which no Englishman of whatever condition can easily entertain (*EL*, 916).

The English, it seems, must cope with an empirical condition that it cannot overcome: geographical environment. The appeal here is singularly planted on the premise that America possesses greater potential for growth than England. When Emerson said this to Carlyle, however, one might argue that it was perhaps America's only or most potent advantage. As a representative of New England, Emerson was forced to be both polite and honest in his engagement with a representative of Old England, in the figure of Carlyle. From the twenty-first century, Emerson's appraisal may seem hubristic, but in the context of his mid-nineteenth century conversation, it was more a sign of a personal (and perhaps a national) inferiority complex.

Deciphering English traits, therefore, was not so out of place, since it was a genealogical method for explaining (a significant) portion of America to itself. Even Americans who did not "come from" England, as it were, were Anglicized—either (and if only) by the language (in speech or in the Bible), or by some form of custom or habit of mind. The experiment of Emerson's book, if not its impetus, was to dissect and catalogue some segments of English life knowing well that that opening and ordering would be relevant to an America trying to explain itself to itself. A dozen years earlier, in his "Address on the Emancipation of the Negroes in the British West Indies," Emerson used English action to help catalyze American action in the cause for the emancipation of Africans held as slaves in America (see *EA*). *English Traits* is decidedly less vitriolic, less overtly political than the "Address," but it nevertheless does not recede from the suggestion that much—if as much by error as insight—can be learned from a study of the English.

Still, again, these English "traits" were not posed as assuredly sanguine in all respects to the American blood and brood. Emerson's cultural genetics was also, to be sure, manifested because of personal experience in the land. The book's first two chapters are submitted as journal-based reviews of his time in England. If Emerson recognizes something of America and Americans from his trips to England, it is only because he recognizes something of himself there first.

The Poet's Eye

The first words of each essay (from *Essays: First Series* and *Essays: Second Series*) are not prose—they are verse. And these epigrammatic stanzas are not borrowed lines from one or another writer. They are Emerson's. Whether the title of the essay is "Spiritual Laws" or "Politics," "The Over-Soul" or "Gifts," poetry is placed as the site of first encounter.

Emerson kept poetry notebooks early on, adding to his collection and revising it at constant intervals. This was as much the case when he was a teenage Harvard student as when he was a minister, and, of course, later when he wrote outside of the academy and the church. Emerson's first book of poetry, entitled *Poems*, appeared in 1847. In 1867, a second volume was published: *May-Day and Other Pieces*. The third and final book of poems to appear in Emerson's life, *Selected Poems*, was printed in 1876. The work from *Poems* is charged with undeniable emotional intensity. Appearing in the wake of both books of *Essays*, these verses seem an exploded version of those miniatures set as the faceplates to so many lines of prose. The varied subjects bear evidence of Emerson's diverse reading, his admitted influences, and his favored symbols: "The Sphinx," "The Humble-Bee," "Woodnotes," "Bacchus," and "Saadi." *May-Day and Other Pieces* begins with two long poems—"May-Day" and "The Adirondacs." By contrast, there are several briefer poems, such as "Brahma," "Days," and "Waldeinsamkeit," that sustain their size by virtue of their balanced concentration. These shorter poems, much like the epigraph poems, seem reduced to essential elements—as if puddles distilled from oceans. *Selected Poems*, appearing in Emerson's waning years, included eight new poems, but was mainly comprised of poems already printed in the first two books.

Emerson wrote poetry, but he also wrote about poetry, about poets, and about the process of writing poems. In "The Poet" (the first essay from *Essays: Second Series*), Emerson codifies what may be taken as a mature synthesis of ideas that had appeared in earlier writing. In his first book, *Nature*, Emerson's affection for ocular metaphor is repeatedly joined with his understanding of poets. Indeed, the principle anxiety of that book is a concern over the poor state of our visual perception, namely, in the sense that we borrow our views of the world from others, from past ages, from books. We look back. The first lines of the introduction read:

> Our age is retrospective. It builds the sepulchers of the fathers. It writes biographies, histories, and criticism. The

foregoing generations beheld God and nature face to face; we, through their eyes. Why should not we also enjoy an original relation to the universe? (*EL*, 7)

An *original* relation does not mean that it will be the first relation, but that it will be a native or personal relation, instead of one adopted or adapted from another. For Emerson, the shift must be from seeing retrospectively to seeing prospectively. The poet is one who can achieve the latter. Emerson illustrates this in a parable about different relations one can have to natural objects (such as a tree), and to the space that such natural objects form (such as the horizon):

> It is this which distinguishes the stick of timber of the wood-cutter, from the tree of the poet. The charming landscape which I saw this morning, is indubitably made up of some twenty or thirty farms. Miller owns this field, Locke that, and Manning the woodland beyond. But none of them owns the landscape. There is a property in the horizon which no man has but he whose eye can integrate all the parts, that is, the poet (*EL*, 9).

Poetical seeing requires that one suppress the habit of instrumentalizing nature, of seeing it always for some mechanical or proprietary purpose. Emerson raises the stakes of this talent of seeing by saying that "to integrate all the parts" one needs to use one's *eye*, that is, one's I, or one's self. This vital doubleness shows the interdependence of visual perception and subjectivity. This lesson reaches its famous caricatured crescendo in *Nature* when Emerson relates his experience of becoming a "transparent eye-ball" (*EL*, 10).

The trail to "The Poet," through poems, essays, and lectures, is strewn with visual metaphor. Nearly each time the eye or seeing is invoked, it is used to reinforce the grounding claim that the way we see the world is intimately connected with the way we are, and how we create. But, in the case of the poet or the scholar, seeing is the proper business. Seeing is what the poet or scholar *does*. In "The American Scholar," regarding the scholar's "duties," he says: "He is one, who raises himself from private considerations, and breathes and lives on public and illustrious thoughts. He is the world's eye" (*EL*, 63).

When Emerson adduces the "nature and functions of the Poet," in the essay "The Poet," he aims to show both by positive illustration and by contrast, what the poet is and what he is good for (*EL*, 448). The poet "interprets" nature and then conveys that view with words—the poet says what the poet sees. The value of the poet resides, then, in his or her potential affect upon our perception of nature, an influence that can deliver a kind of liberation. Thus Emerson comments on the latent force of reading a poem:

> And now my chains are to be broken; I shall mount above these clouds and opaque airs in which I live,—opaque, though they seem transparent,—and from the heaven of truth I shall see and comprehend my relations. That will reconcile me to life, and renovate nature, to see trifles animated by a tendency, and to know what I am doing (*EL*, 451).

This is a grand burden for a poet to bear, and Emerson admits, such exaltation and clarity is as rare as it is fantastic. Therefore, we cannot remain idle and despondent while the poet prepares some verse for our aid. And few people actually do such waiting. Emerson sees this as principle evidence that poetry happens by symbols or signs, not just by words (*EL*, 452-3, and see Ch. IV of *Nature*).

> Who loves nature? Who does not? Is it only poets, and men of leisure and cultivation, who live with her? No; but also hunters, farmers, grooms, and butchers, though they express their affection in their choice of life, and not in their choice of words (*EL*, 453).

"The people fancy they hate poetry, and they are all poets and mystics!" (*EL*, 454). We are not enlightened to our potency as poets because the habit is to make the Poet's poems the benchmark for poetic expression and perception. Emerson tells us that the poets are indeed our "liberating gods," but that should not disenfranchise the rest from seeing poetically (*EL*, 461-2).

> We are symbols, and inhabit symbols; workman, work, and tools, words and things, birth and death, all are emblems (*EL*, 456).

How many (or, how few) perceive their work—whatever its sort—*as poetry*? How many privilege straight lines of verse over straight lumber? The poet does not dispossess us of our capacity for poetry; the poet reminds us of it. The poet "perceives the independence of the thought on the symbol, the stability of the thought, the accidency and fugacity of the symbol" (*Ibid.*). The poet is a liberator of perception, helping us to see how the symbols we use to account for the world are mobile, and many-layered. The poet "admits us to a new scene" so that we may admit the new that is seen.

5

Constituting an Aesthetic for the Conduct of Life

Between the bookends of publishing *The Conduct of Life* in 1860 and *Society and Solitude* in 1870, Emerson worked to fulfill the expectation that his status had enlarged. This decade, his last active and productive one, finds him still fervently pressing his views on abolition and other social causes, traveling widely throughout the United States by train to give lectures, meeting with Abraham Lincoln and walking with Walt Whitman, and beginning to address Americans in a last plea of exhortation to ideas familiar, but still relevant, from his first essays.

From the late 1830's, Emerson had established himself as a writer who speaks, that is, a writer who brings his ideas out of the study into a public realm for scrutiny. This engagement, as much pointed to the mechanic and farmer as to the politician and professor, developed with even more intensity in Civil War era lectures such as "American Civilization" (1862) and "Fortune of the Republic" (1864). In these presentations, and in his essays, Emerson developed a more overt blend of social and political criticism. He relied increasingly on proximate events and historical examples to reinforce his message. And the sentiment that ethics grounds all personal and public life seems appended to every sentence.

It should be difficult to defend the view that Emerson spent his mature years sequestered in his study on Lexington Road in Concord reading Plutarch all afternoon and writing essays in the evening after supper (though he did write an introduction to *Plutarch's Morals* in 1870). Surely, this was part of the scene. But the portrait should also include him traveling by train to Toronto (1860), Washington, D.C.

(1862), Minnesota and Iowa (1867); addressing the Massachusetts Anti-Slavery Society (1861); reviewing the U.S. cadets at West Point (1863) and overseeing students at Harvard College (1867); being elected to the Academy of Arts and Sciences (1864); and, of great symbolic importance—returning to deliver the Phi Beta Kappa oration at Harvard (1867), nearly three decades after presenting "The American Scholar" (1837).

Emerson's earliest critical remarks, even those from sermons written while a parish minister, evidence a continuity of regard for the necessity of reform in human life. Indeed, the grounding concern for individual integrity remained—throughout his works—the perception that others are too quickly and easily satisfied with the status quo. Imbued with such complacency, individuals deprive themselves of a necessary dynamism—a movement that is everywhere shown in natural systems. Change and revision as much as regeneration and decay are principles of nature that ought to be heeded in human life. This is perhaps no more apparent than in religion and politics where the ossification of belief is a hallmark of piety (in the former) and loyalty (in the latter). Throughout his career, Emerson encouraged the risk that accompanies a critical inheritance of long-standing faiths and policies. His invocations to risk and reform occupy a privileged place in his writings. But those writings also stand as instances of *his* trials of risk and reform. It is then in the way Emerson undergoes such experiments, that we are submitted to his response to stagnancy. Such a methodology—with all its drama, failure, and inspiration—is exceptionally well-defined in Emerson's confrontation with three of the dominant reform issues of his time: the emancipation of slaves, rights for Native Americans, and women's suffrage. His reports on these tumultuous issues, we should by now expect, were based on underlying ethical presentments that to be human means, in large measure, working out one's capacity for change, and thus, the scope of individual freedom.

Fate's Freedom

In 1842, in a lecture—"The Transcendentalist"—read at the Masonic Temple in Boston, Emerson said: "Now every one must do after his kind, be he asp or angel, and these must. The question, which a wise man and a student of modern history will ask, is, what that kind is?" (*EL*, 199). The year before, in "Self-Reliance," he declared: "But do your work, and I shall know you. Do your work, and you shall reinforce yourself" (*EL*, 264). But, one may plead—"What is *my* work?"—doubting not just that there is work to be done, but that such activity may be self-possessed. By the time Emerson wrote the above, he had already spent a decade's worth of anxieties over his proper vocation. These anxieties are sustained throughout his life, as if a winding coil tracing the perimeter of an immoveable core. The durability of the question—"what is *my* work?"—does not instance a failure of will or imagination, but a confrontation with an enigmatic aspect of human conduct. Emerson was not aiming to solve this query, but to resolve himself to its abiding presence.

On the boat ride home from England in 1833, having begun to draft *Nature*, he wrote in his journal: "I like my book about nature & wish I knew where & how I ought to live" (September 6, 1833. *EJ*, 116). It is not difficult to imagine a thirty-year old confessing a worry about what work should be done, and how it ought to be carried out. And yet, when Emerson is fifty-seven, in 1860, he writes—in the first paragraph of the second essay of *The Conduct of Life*—of the same question, of the same doubt:

> To me, however, the question of the times resolved itself into a practical question of the conduct of life. How shall I live? (*EL*, 943)

The obscure Emerson aboard his homeward bound ship in 1833, and the luminous Emerson writing at the zenith of his established and revered career in 1860, asks the *same* question. It is, of course, not his question. It is a guiding question of ancient Greek philosophy, and perhaps *the* question of Stoic philosophy, both of which Emerson was deeply familiar with. There is thus much intrigue in the claim that the question of Emerson's time is a question that was not (just) of his time. In much the same way that the young and the old Emerson were asking about work, about how to live, so the question of "the times" becomes a question for all time. The "practical question of the conduct of life" is not an affair solely of Roman orators or emperors, or of nineteenth-century New England preachers, poets, and philosophers: it is a *human* question.

All this, however, presupposes the freedom of human agency. If one is not free, the question "How shall I live?" is neutralized. It need not be asked because there is no means of responding to it, much less of answering it. To commence his essay "Fate" with this question, therefore, sets Emerson to a ambitious task: in what way can we understand the limitations that constrain human life so that there is yet room enough to mount a reply to *the* question? The stakes of this venture are high indeed, as the imposition of fate would dissolve the possibility of human formation (e.g., choosing work, deciding how to live), and the promise of human reformation (e.g., remaking life through a process of experiment). If one is fated, there is neither ground for responsibility to oneself, nor to others. Individual and social projects of formation and reformation are undermined, and so the exhortations found in "Self-Reliance" and "Man the Reformer" are spoken to a dream world where there is a self to rely on, and a human life capable of reform. Emerson's investigation in "Fate" is to come to terms with the "irresistible dictation" that would preclude comprehension of how "necessity does compert with liberty" (*EL*, 943).

Emerson says that "The book of Nature is the book of Fate," and that fate is "known to us as limitation" (*EL*, 949, 952). The query, then, is to what extent the human is bound by nature. At first, Emerson supposes that "even thought itself is not about Fate," and for this reason: "In its last and loftiest ascensions, insight itself, and the freedom of the will, is one of its obedient members" (*EL*, 952-3). But this, he surmises, does not sufficiently account for the way in which human life works its way through nature, in nature:

> For, though Fate is immense, so is power, which is the other fact in the dual world, immense. If Fate follows and limits power, power attends and antagonizes Fate. . . . Man is not order of nature, sack and sack, belly and members, link in a chain, nor ignominious baggage, but a stupendous antagonism (*EL*, 953).

The human is possessed of a "power" that can respond to nature, and its edicts—that is, the force of its laws. "If there be omnipotence in the stroke, there is omnipotence of recoil" (*EL*, 954). Nature's causes are not final since the human has the power to affect or interpret or respond to that dictation. Drawing heavily upon Stoic sentiments, Emerson avows that the human power to front fate has mainly to do with a cognitive disposition, from which practical action in the world can follow:

> To hazard the contradiction,—freedom is necessary. If you please to plant yourself on the side of Fate, and say, Fate is all; then we say, a part of Fate is the freedom of man. Forever wells up the impulse of choosing and acting in the soul. Intellect annuls Fate. So far as a man thinks, he is free (*EL*, 953).

Thinking, therefore, is the process by which nature or fate's "dictation" is annulled. Decades earlier, in his Phi Beta Kappa oration, "The American Scholar," he said that "the scholar is the delegated intellect. In the right state, he is, *Man Thinking*" (*EL*, 54. Emerson's italics). And in "Self-Reliance," he continued his taxonomy of cognitive powers when he said: "To believe your own thought, to believe that what is true for you in your private heart is true for all men,—that is genius. Speak your latent conviction, and it shall be the universal sense; for the inmost in due time becomes the outmost. . ." (*EL*, 259). Man Thinking, the scholar (or "delegated intellect"), or genius all bear the mark of freedom. Declaring one's "latent conviction" derives from "the impulse of choosing and acting," and so shows that the inmost (freedom of one's thoughts) enters the realm of the outmost (the fate of nature).

Emerson's logic is not high-handed, but practical. He infers that most humans are "slaves" because they "have never dared to think or to act" (*EL*, 954). This pathetic circumstance is shown by the majority of humans—those who are stunned and paralyzed by the imposition of fate. They do not mount a "stupendous antagonism" to nature; they are merely stupefied. "But the dogma [of Destiny or fate] makes a different impression, when it is held by the weak and lazy. 'Tis weak and vicious people who cast the blame on Fate" (*Ibid.*).

Humans are not to use fate as an excuse for thinking and acting, but as its prime incentive. "The right use of Fate is to bring up our conduct to the loftiness of nature" (*Ibid.*). The Stoics taught the doctrine of *amor fati*—the love of fate. This did not compromise their actions, nor did it invite them to despair of thought's efficacy. Emerson admires the affection of the Stoical attitude—their "loving resignation," their "fatal courage"—because it shows the power of intellect that resides in Man Thinking, in the scholar, in he or she who retains self-trust in his or her genius (*Ibid.*). "If you believe in Fate to your harm, believe it, at least, for your good" (*Ibid.*). This tragic optimism reinforces one's approach to confronting "fate with fate," that is, living with the burden that "freedom is necessary"—meaning *both* that it is fated, and that it must be exercised in order to raise one to the pedigree of the human (*Ibid.*).

In "Fate," Emerson makes a bid to explain how he figures a free thought can issue a free act, that is, how by following one's genius (like Socrates' daimon) the power of will is expressed in the context of nature. Emerson's writing, therefore, *is* an act of confronting fate with fate, *is* an exercise of his dictation against the dictation nature supplies. But like the Stoics, Emerson saw how a worded treatise is deprived of its force when its influence ceases at the margins of the page. The incentive to thinking must exceed these limits too. In the decades leading up to the composition of "Fate," there are numerous instances in which Emerson transgresses the limits of the page by thinking and acting in the context of immanent crises of human conduct.

> Fate involves the melioration. . . . Behind every individual, closes organization: before him, opens liberty,—the Better, the Best. . . . Liberation of the will from the sheaths and clogs of organization which he has outgrown, is the end and aim of this world. Every calamity is a spur and valuable hint; and where his endeavors do not yet fully avail, they tell as tendency (*EL*, 960).

Emerson wrote this on the eve of the Civil War. This domestic calamity would be a "spur and valuable hint" to America long after Appomattox. In the middle of the nineteenth-century, Emerson was already monitoring the "tendency" that could not be denied, namely, the promulgation and then extension of human freedom. It is now frightfully obvious the degree to which the *liberty* of some humans depends on the *choice* of others. Recognizing the freedom of African-Americans, Native Americans, and women, shows the terrifying extent to which Emerson's three word declaration rings valid: "Intellect annuls Fate." Humans, to be sure, must face the dictations of nature, but to a more vital degree, humans must face their own dictations. To think that a human is free is to make him so.

Addressing Slavery, Redressing the Human

In antebellum New England, slavery, which separated North from South, also proved divisive for local constituencies. In Massachusetts, the question of abolition reached a fever pitch in the decades leading up to the Civil War. Emerson's participation in this debate was precipitated by the influence of British abolition, potential changes in American political geography, and his conceptions of race and reform. How best to *enact* reform remained a dominant theme of his writing.

Being an abolitionist entailed more than being anti-slavery. An abolitionist needed to have a firm commitment to substantive reformation (in word and deed) of the domestic policy regarding institutional slavery. Emerson was not among the first to speak out against slavery, but when he did, beginning fervently in the late 1830's, his oratory and argument fit deservingly within the most revolutionary abolitionists, a group that included William Lloyd Garrison [1805-

1879], Wendell Phillips [1811-1884], Theodore Parker [1810-1860], Horace Greeley [1811-1872], John Greenleaf Whittier [1807-1892], and Frederick Douglass [1817-1895]. His initial hesitation to participate gave way to a duty-bound commitment to the cause, which, for him, hinged on individual action (*EA*, xii, xx).

In 1833, the British abolitionists succeeded in emancipating the slaves of the British West Indies. This event became a pivotal mark, which catalyzed Emerson's resolve to address the problem of slavery in America in the years to come. His scorn was that much more incited for the contrast now established between those freed by the British, and those who remained enslaved under the United States:

> I said, this event is signal in the history of human civilization. There are many styles of civilization, and not one only. Ours is full of barbarities. There are many faculties in man, each of which takes its turn of activity, and that faculty which is paramount in any period, and exerts itself through the strongest nation, determines the civility of that age; and each age thinks its own the perfection of reason. Our culture is very cheap and intelligible (*EA*, 19).

The "strongest nation," in the mid-1840s, was England, and it had set the precedent America ought to follow. America's civility as much as its civilization depended on such an emulation. " . . . [T]he civility of no race can be perfect whilst another race is degraded. It is a doctrine alike of the oldest, and of the newest philosophy, that, man is one, and that you cannot injure any member, without a sympathetic injury to all the members (*EA*, 32).

Another catalyzing force was the proposed annexation of Texas into the Union in 1837. Emerson was "decidedly hostile" to the annex, and saw it as a direct assault upon the free states, whose power, he feared, would be overcome by the growth of the slaveholding states to a majority (*EA*, xxvii). While England had freed its slaves, it seemed America was poised not just to keep its slaves, but also to multiply their population. Emerson would have to find his own method for contributing to the end of slavery on his native soil. It was not good enough to simply join a group; one had to be a group unto oneself.

Emerson saw reform as one of the few essential and natural duties of man. In the same season that "Self-Reliance" appeared, Emerson wrote, in his lecture "Man the Reformer," that "We are to revise the whole of our social structure, the state, the school, religion, marriage, trade, science, and explore their foundations in our own nature" (*EL*,

146). This *re-vision* is just that: a call to look at things anew, and decide which align with our current beliefs, which are objectionable, and then *act* accordingly. He continued: "What is a man born for but to be a Reformer, a Re-maker of what man has made; a renouncer of lies; restorer of truth and good. . . ?" (*EL*, 146) What else is slavery but one of those man-made lies that we ought to revise?

As might be expected, Emerson's strategy for *social* reform lay squarely on *individual* reform. That is, he held the individual, in his or her personal conduct, culpable for the broader range of societal ills. Though slavery ended in Massachusetts in 1780, it continued in other forms, as there were pernicious remnants of it in citizens' commerce with slaveholders. Emerson pointed out the hypocrisy, and lined his words with evidence of these contradictions between belief and action. "The sugar they raised was excellent: nobody tasted the blood in it" (*EA*, 20).

Emerson was very early on convinced of the equality of humankind, whether white or black, male of female. He did not see his political action framed by the specter of white helping black, and not even by a man helping another man. Rather, Emerson energized his vitriolic speech by confessions of conscience; as he did when protesting the sanctity of the Eucharist in 1832, Emerson appealed primarily to an internal well-spring of validation. He spoke on his own behalf as a man, and how slavery offended him personally. This was coupled with a talent for persuasion, and his appeal to the "moral sense" of his audience (*EA*, 21). That is not to say that Emerson neglected, or was not aware of, the status of slaves as black. It was precisely because *blackness* was the criterion for slavery that he found the holding of these men, women, and children so indefensible. Granted, he also insisted that there are *no* good reasons for keeping slaves (". . . it is cheaper to pay wages, than to own the slave."—and that is just an economic fact, not a moral one (*EA*, 8)). But keeping them because they are black, is plainly ludicrous: ". . . none but a stupid or a malignant person can hesitate on a view of the facts" (*Ibid.*). The "facts" are that race, according to Emerson, is a function of history and culture, and not a matter of intellectual, moral, or spiritual power. Race is a contingent and superficial difference, not an ontologically necessary or informative one. The argument against racial injustice is thus (literally) within each of us: "The blood is moral: the blood is anti-slavery" (*EA*, 10). Emerson endorsed the idea that "men of all colors have equal rights in law, and an equal footing in society" (*EA*, 19). The abolition movement, Emerson contended, contributes to "the annihilation of the old indecent nonsense about the nature of the negro" as inferior to whites (*EA*, 29). Race is merely an idea, not a fact of nature: "Here is the anti-slave: here is man: and if you have man, black or white is an insignificance" (*EA*, 31).

Because Emerson was a celebrity whose star so many abolitionists desired to pin on their banners, and because he was so suspicious of joining groups, Emerson was allowed to enact his method of reform as he wished: by giving speeches, by appealing to moral sense, and by championing the liberation of individual genius. In a lecture given at Amory Hall in 1844, entitled "New England Reformers," he correlated the expression of genius to the possibility of freedom. In this context, he suspected his audience was mentally incarcerated. In the context of a critique of slavery, however, the passage takes on another valence of urgency:

> Obedience to his genius is the only liberating influence. We wish to escape from subjection, and a sense of inferiority,—we make self-denying ordinances, we drink water, we eat grass, we refuse the laws, we go to jail: it is all in vain; only by obedience to his genius; only by the freest activity in the way constitutional to him, does an angel seem to arise before a man, and lead him by the hand out of all the wards of the prison (*EP*, 233).

The First Amendment becomes the keystone of social action because it reinforces individual speech. With that right secured, genius may be heeded without interference, that is, without excuse. *This* freedom (of speech) would be the enabling force for achieving *that* freedom (of slaves). After all, emancipation was finally achieved by a *proclamation*. In response to the Compromise of 1850, Emerson wrote that in such an instance of felt offense it is permissible (at the least) to protest "by voice and by pen . . . against the detestable statute of the last congress" (*EA*, xxxix). Yet, as his earlier remarks remind, such transgression is only viable if one follows one's genius. Emerson was a social reformer on private terms who sought to revise action by putting the weight of an entire institution on the shoulders of each individual.

Native America, American Natives

In the spring of 1838, the Cherokee Indians, who once occupied nearly forty thousand square miles of territory, but who had been reduced to about four thousand, were on the verge of being dispossessed of even that portion (Richardson, 276). Under the precedents set by Andrew Jackson, the newly elected President Martin Van Buren propelled orders to have the Cherokees relocated to land west of the Mississippi River. Constituencies of protest grew nationwide, especially among those already fiercely embroiled in the cause for abolition—as yet more evidence for their arguments exposing injustices. The fervor and outrage among New England reformers was especially high as this policy reinforced not only the transgression of law (a political claim), but also the abusive treatment of human beings (a moral claim).

On March 12, 1838, Emerson gave a speech entitled "The Peace Principle" (later, ironically re-titled "War") in which he outlined a genealogy of war that shows how humans are moving (however slowly) toward peace. If humans will mature, for example, by adapting to the implicated responsibilities of self-possession, then peace can be justifiably regarded as an inevitability. When we puzzle over why there is slavery, dislocation and destitution of the Native American, and oppression of women, we ask questions of ourselves, about our own responsibilities to humankind.

> Every nation and every man instantly surround themselves with a material apparatus which exactly corresponds to their moral state, or their state of thought. Observe how every truth and every error, each a *thought* of some man's mind, clothes itself with societies, houses, cities, language, ceremonies, newspapers. Observe the ideas of the present day,—orthodoxy, skepticism, missions, popular education, temperance, anti-masonry, anti-slavery; see how each of these abstractions has embodied itself in an imposing apparatus in the community; and how timber, brick, lime and stone have flown into convenient shape, obedient to the master-idea reigning in the minds of many persons (*CW*, vol. XI, 164).

Social ethics and cultural institutions are the embodiments of ideas—thoughts that are clothed. The warmonger, fit in his current state but drawn to another, might ask of peace: "How is it to pass out of thoughts into things?" (*CW*, vol. XI, 170). Emerson perceived the reply in evolutionary terms:

> For the only hope of this cause is in the increased insight, and it is to be accomplished by the spontaneous teaching, of the cultivated soul, in its secret experience and meditation,—that it is now time that it should pass out of the state of beast into the state of man (*CW*, vol. XI, 171).

A month later, on April 23, 1838, he wrote a letter to President Van Buren in which his abstract protest was put to work in an immanent example. Where "The Peace Principle" progressed mainly by a rhetorical appeal to the self-dependence of the human—"men who have, by their intellectual insight or else by their moral elevation, attained such a perception of their own intrinsic worth that they do not think property or their own body a sufficient good to be saved by such a dereliction of principle as treating a man like a sheep"—this open-letter—published only a month before the Trail of Tears began—aimed, by din of moral and legal appeal, to illustrate how despicable such treatment would be, and how direly its exercise would reflect upon the character of the American soul (*CW*, vol. XI, 174).

In his letter to the President of the United States, Emerson began by clarifying a legal fact, namely, that almost ninety percent of the Cherokee nation objected to the treaty signed with the government by a few Cherokee dissenters. For this reason, the legal justification for the removal of this people is based on a "sham treaty" (*EA*, 2). Emerson makes Van Buren's temptation to honor this sham the condition for shame. But the legal complaint only brews to moral outrage once it is set upon the stronger ground of ethical infraction. The government, Emerson argued, in following out a transgression against the Cherokee is in danger of committing a transgression against the people of the United States.

> We hoped the Indians were misinformed, and their remonstrance was premature, and would turn out to be a needless act of terror. The piety, the principle, that is left in these United States—if only its coarsest form, a regard to the speech of men—forbid us to entertain it as a fact. Such a dereliction of all faith and virtue, such a denial of justice, and such deafness to screams for mercy, were never heard of in times of peace, and in the dealing of a nation with its own allies and wards, since the earth was made (*EA*, 3).

Emerson is sending his word to Van Burn as an admonition. "A crime is projected that confounds our understandings by its magnitude—a crime that really deprives us as well as the Cherokees of a country" (*Ibid.*). Such action would be a blight on "national and human justice" and "stink to the world" (*Ibid.*). Alas, we know that Emerson's letter, and those on whose behalf it spoke, failed to rally the "moral sentiment" of the country's leader to honor the Cherokee, and by that measure, the American people. On May 23, 1838 the Cherokees were put out, and with that "all the attributes of reason, of civility, of justice, and even of mercy . . . [were] put off" (*EA*, 4).

Woman; Sameness, and (the) Difference

William Emerson, Emerson's father, died in 1811, when the young Emerson was just shy of turning eight. During his adolescence, it would be Emerson's mother—Ruth Haskins Emerson—and his brilliant, doting aunt Mary Moody Emerson, who would provide the dual conditions from which Emerson summoned an early intellectual maturity. Emerson was duly indebted to his mother for making it possible for him, and his brothers (Edward, William, and Charles) to attend Harvard College. But it was self-educated Mary who prodded young Waldo to surmise her high degree of conceptual acumen and to meet her expectations for his own. This was achieved partly through conversation, but also through correspondence.

Upon returning from Europe in 1833, and as he began to establish a new circle of peers, Emerson developed deep and lasting friendships with Caroline Sturgis, Elizabeth Palmer Peabody, Elizabeth Hoar, and, Margaret Fuller. To Emerson, these women were formidable intellects possessed of rare and admirable gifts. He listened to them, conversed with them, wrote about them and to them, and sustained their strong influences upon him.

In 1848 a Woman's Rights Convention was held in Seneca Falls, New York. Just as British emancipation of its West Indian colonies, and the United States government treatment of Cherokees, stimulated Emerson to abolition and the securing of Native American rights, so had this gathering created a felt obligation to respond to the state of women in America, and elsewhere. In 1850, when another Women's Rights Convention convened in Worcester, Massachusetts, Emerson sent his support for the principles there argued for. And in 1855, at another meeting of the Women's Rights Convention, Emerson attended and addressed the delegation in unambiguously supportive terms. The lecture was later revised as the essay "Woman," in which he states that the involvement of women in the cause for abolition proved to be "a great scholar" for educating the human about humanity. "There was nothing it did not pry into, no right it did not explore, no wrong it did not expose" (*CW*, vol. XI, 416). The moral urgency for revising the world of women, therefore could be delineated from revising the world of the slave. In hearing women speak for the abolition of slavery, one was faced with an overt, but widely suppressed, contradiction. To confirm what women abolitionists said of slavery meant to confirm what men should say of women, namely, that *another* domain of emancipation is morally necessary. Arguments for the abolition of slaves—by women—hastened thoughts of women's emancipation from a diminished existential status. This revision, in turn, opened new valuations of moral, political, and social positions. As with African-Americans, the rights of women, were no longer seen as given, but as made. This, Emerson thought, was as laudable as it was inevitable, as deserved as it was beneficial.

> One truth leads in another by the hand; one right is an accession of strength to take more. And the times are marked by the new attitude of Woman; urging, by argument and by association, her rights of all kinds,—in short, to one half of the world;—as the right to education, to avenues of employment, to equal rights of property, to equal rights of marriage, to the exercise of the professions and of suffrage (*CW*, vol. XI, 416).

Emerson's alliance to the cause of women's rights is here unambiguous, but there are occasions when his language can sound—to our ears—to condescend to women. If that is so, it is because he works to revise the terms by which women are known through familiar language. And so we hear him speak of "affection" and "sentiment," and "love," but these terms are deployed *not* to reinforce long-held prejudices. Rather, these are words that Emerson holds in highest esteem for the *human*. Acknowledge how familiar they are to his many prior writings. That he views women as the privileged possessors and executors of these elements makes them that much more, well, human. Emerson anticipates even *our* suspicions of his view by dwelling on the characterization of women in Aristophanes, Rabelais, and Tennyson:

> In all, the body of the joke is one, namely, to charge women with temperament; to describe them as victims of temperament; and is identical with Mahomet's opinion that women have not a sufficient moral or intellectual force to control the perturbations of their physical structure. These were all drawings of morbid anatomy, and such satire as might be written on the tenants of a hospital or on an asylum for idiots (*CW*, vol. XI, 417).

Again, any student of "Experience" will recognize that "temperament" is not a word Emerson wishes to associate with women, but with the human condition. And it is hardly a damnable aspect of our lives: we are not so much its "victims" as its victors. It is a superstition to believe that if women came into possession of expanded rights they would somehow be unhinged from their prior selves, as if "they cannot enter this arena without being contaminated and unsexed" (*CW*, vol. XI, 421). To believe by entering into political and social life (in ways that men have) women would be poisoned and neutered only "shows how barbarous we are,—that our policies are so crooked, made up of things not to be spoken, to be understood only by wink and nudge; this man to be coaxed, that man to be bought, and that other to be duped. It is easy to see that there is contamination enough, but it rots the men now, and fills the air with stench" (*CW*, vol. XI, 423). In such a malodorous climate, Emerson presumed that women would not *want* to join the fetid affair—though he believed the presence of women would duly disinfect the air of such stagnancy. But, he reasoned, their inclusion and participation is (or should be) their choice. "I do not think it yet appears that women wish this equal share in public affairs. But it is they and not we that are to determine it" (*CW*, vol. XI, 424). Emerson treads the moral, the political, and the emotional reasons for repudiating these denials to women, but perhaps best strikes the exigency of the issue when putting in parallel the declared independence of America from Britain and that of women from men: "If you do refuse them a vote, you will also refuse to tax them,—according to our Teutonic principle, No representation, no tax" (*Ibid.*). One wishes to have the choice to be represented, and perhaps even more so, to be (a) representative.

Almost a decade before Lincoln's Emancipation, Emerson pleaded that "When new opinions appear, they will be entertained and respected, by every fair mind, according to their reasonableness, and not according to their convenience, or their fitness to shock our customs" (*Ibid.*). It is with the rights of Woman as with the freedom of African-Americans that habits of belief ought not to interfere with the possibilities of revision. This path is marked by an abiding respect for the weight of following out its implications—"not by the way of manufacturing public opinion, which lapses continually into expediency, and makes charlatans" (*CW*, vol. XI, 425).

In many ways, the women who surrounding Emerson—his wives Ellen and Lidian; Fuller, Sturgis, Hoar, Peabody; and his aunt Mary—prefigure his convictions for abolition and women's rights. Their opinions have come to light through his work and words, even as they were capably announced in and through their own voices (in letters, journals, essays, books, and speeches). In tracing this genealogy of influence, then, it is not unwarranted to see their effect upon those who took to Emerson's call, and who adopted him as an ally. Many of the beacons of Woman's Suffrage—Elizabeth Cady

Stanton, Julia Ward Howe, and Ednah Dow Cheney (leader of the Massachusetts Woman Suffrage Society)—paid him the compliment of designating him a worthy reference, and a genuine advocate of their cause (Garvey, 106). However, the still largely unacknowledged ground upon and out of which this movement emerged is Margaret Fuller and her seminal *Women in the Nineteenth Century*. Emerson's ideas emanate the influence of this book, as Emerson sustained the impact of its author.

6

Eminent Estimations:
An Encomium

It may be considered spurious to defend or evaluate an artist's reputation by consulting the opinions of other artists, not so much because they lack talent for criticism, but because the idea of opinion as argument (even if inductive) is insufficiently convincing. The admonition is clearly to avoid, when possible, committing the genetic fallacy, viz., asserting truth based on the authority of a source. Questioning the authority of inherited valuations is the commonest way of heeding this warning. Nevertheless, we need not trust an opinion in order to be interested in hearing it; we do not have to submit to another's authority to consider his or her assessment. And yet, we might want to do both.

Since the late 1830's, Emerson's writing has been the referent of much quotation, and much criticism. Both practices, despite the content quoted or criticized, implicate Emerson as a touchstone. For this reason, there is an abundance of material with Emerson as its subject. In what follows, I have gathered some remarks on Emerson written by friends and contemporaries, by distant admirers, by proximate critics, and by those who have been influenced by his writing and, in their remarks, lay the ground for others to be so. There is no consensus of opinion, but perhaps only of regard. There is praise and chastisement, apology and ambivalence. If unanimity can be found, it is in the shared task of reckoning with Emerson's work and life.

Margaret Fuller [1810-1850]

You question me as to the nature of the benefits conferred upon me by Mr. E's preaching. I answer, that his influence has been more beneficial to me than that of any American, and that from him I first learned what is meant by an inward life. . . . Several of his sermons stand apart in memory, like landmarks of my spiritual history. It would take a volume to tell what this one influence did for me. But perhaps I shall some time see that it was best for me to be forced to help myself.[1]

* * *

These essays [viz., *Second Series*], it has been justly said, tire like a string of mosaics or a house built of medals. We miss what we expect in the work of the great poet or the great philosopher, the liberal air of all the zones: the glow, uniform yet various in tint, which is given to a body by free circulation of the heart's blood from the hour of birth.[2]

Andrews Norton [1756-1853]

The characteristics of this school [such as Emerson is said to represent] are the most extraordinary assumption, united with great ignorance, and incapacity for reasoning. . . . They announce themselves as the prophets and priests of a new future, in which all is to be changed, all old opinions done away, and all present forms of society abolished. But by what process this joyful revolution is to be effected we are not told; nor how human happiness and virtue is to be saved from the universal wreck, and regenerated in their Medea's caldron. . . .

The rejection of reasoning is accompanied with an equal contempt for good taste. All modesty is laid aside. . . . He continually obtrudes himself upon his reader, and announces his own convictions, as if from their having that character, they were necessarily indisputable. . . .[3]

Henry James [1843-1916]

. . . [B]ut there is even yet a sort of drollery in the spectacle of a body of people among whom the author of *The American Scholar* and of the Address of 1838 at the Harvard Divinity College passed as profane, and who failed to see that he only gave his plea for the spiritual life the advantage of a brilliant expression. They were so provincial as to think that brilliancy came ill recommended, and they were shocked at his ceasing to care for the prayer and the sermon.

They might have perceived that he *was* the prayer and the sermon: not in the least a secularizer, but in his own subtle insinuating way a sanctifier.[4]

* * *

He liked literature as a thing to refer to, liked the very names of which it is full, and used them, especially in his later writings, for purposes of ornament, to dress the dish, sometimes with an unmeasured profusion. I open *The Conduct of Life* and find a dozen on the page. He mentions more authorities than is the fashion to-day. He can easily say, of course, that he follows a better one—that of his well-loved and irrepressibly allusive Montaigne. In his own bookishness there is a certain contradiction, just as there is a latent incompleteness in his whole literary side. Independence, the return to nature, the finding out and doing for oneself, was what he mostly highly recommended; and yet he is constantly reminding his readers of the conventional signs and consecrations—of what other men have done.[5]

William James [1842-1910]

Such a conviction that Divinity is everywhere may easily make of one an optimist of the sentimental type that refuses to speak ill of anything. Emerson's drastic perception of differences kept him at the opposite pole from this weakness. After you have seen men a few times, he could say, you find most of them as alike as their barns and pantries, and soon as musty and dreary. Never was such a fastidious lover of significance and distinction, and never an eye so keen for their discovery.[6]

George Santayana [1863-1952]

The source of his power lay not in his doctrine, but in his temperament, and the rare quality of his wisdom was due less to his reason than to his imagination. Reality eluded him; he had neither diligence nor constancy enough to master and possess it; but his mind was open to all philosophic influences, from whatever quarter they might blow; the lessons of science and the hints of poetry worked themselves out in him to a free and personal religion. He differed from the plodding man, not in knowing things better, but in having more ways of knowing them.[7]

Elizabeth Palmer Peabody [1804-1894]

And to his own solution, some say he is unintelligible, talks darkly. They do not seem to have observed that he says nothing in the way of solution, so that nothing can be darkly said. This is what has disappointed the best lovers of his book. But if he does not give his own solution of the enigma, he does what is next best, he tells us the condition of solving it ourselves.[8]

Friedrich Nietzsche [1845-1900]

Emerson.—Much more enlightened, venturesome, complex, refined than Carlyle; above all, happier . . . The sort of man who instinctively feeds only on ambrosia, who leaves behind whatever is indigestible in things. In comparison to Carlyle, a man of taste.—Carlyle, who loved him very much, nevertheless said of him: "he does not give *us* enough to chew on"—which he may have been right to say, but not to Emerson's disadvantage.—Emerson has that good-natured and brilliant cheerfulness that deters all seriousness; he simply does not know how old he already is and how young he will still be—he could say of himself, in the words of Lope de Vega, "*yo me sucedo a mi mismo*" [I am my own successor]. His spirit always finds reasons to be content and even thankful; and on occasion he approaches the cheerful transcendence of that worthy man who came back from an amorous tryst *tamquam re bene gesta* [as if the deed had been well done]. "*Ut desint vires,*" he said thankfully, "*tamen est laudanda voluptas*" [Though the power is lacking, the lust is to be praised]."[9]

Matthew Arnold [1822-1888]

And, in truth, one of the legitimate poets, Emerson, in my opinion, is not. His poetry is interesting, it makes one think; but it is not the poetry of one of the born poets. . . .
. . . But I go further, and say that I do not place him among the great writers, the great men of letters. . . .
. . . Emerson cannot, I think, be called with justice a great philosophical writer. He cannot build; his arrangement of philosophical ideas has no progress in it, no evolution; he does not construct a philosophy. . . .
. . . We have not in Emerson a great poet, a great writer, a great philosophy-maker. His relation to us is not one of those personages; yet it is a relation of, I think, even superior importance. His relation to

us is more like that of the Roman Emperor Marcus Aurelius. Marcus Aurelius is not a great writer, a great philosophy-maker; he is the friend and aider of those who would live in the spirit. Emerson is the same. He is the friend and aider of those who would live in the spirit. . . .[10]

* * *

As Wordsworth's poetry is, in my judgment, the most important work done in verse, in our language, during the present century, so Emerson's "Essays" are, I think, the most important work done in prose.[11]

John Dewey [1859-1952]

It is said that Emerson is not a philosopher. . . . But to make this short, I am not acquainted with any writer, no matter how assured his position in treatises upon the history of philosophy, whose movement of thought is more compact and unified, nor one who combines more adequately diversity of intellectual attack with concentration of form and effect. . . . The condescending patronage by literary critics of Emerson's lack of cohesiveness may remind us that philosophers have no monopoly on this particular form of stupidity.[12]

Virginia Woolf [1864-1938]

Emerson, born among half-taught people, in a new land, kept always the immature habit of conceiving that a man is made up of separate qualities, which can be separately developed and praised. It is a belief necessary to schoolmasters; and to some extent Emerson is always a schoolmaster, making the world very simple for his scholars, a place of discipline and reward. But this simplicity, which is in his diaries as well as in his finished works—for he was not to be "found out"—is the result not only of ignoring so much, but of such concentration upon a few things. By means of it he can produce an extraordinary effect of exaltation. . . . But these exaltations are not practicable; they will not stand interruption. Where shall we lay the blame? Is he too simple, or are we too worn? But the beauty of his view is great, because it can rebuke us, even while we feel that he does not understand.[13]

Walt Whitman [1819-1892]

First, then, these pages are perhaps too perfect, too concentrated. (How good, for instance, is good butter, good sugar. But to be eating nothing but sugar and butter all the time! even if ever so good.) And though the author has much to say of freedom and wildness and simplicity and spontaneity, no performance was ever more based on artificial scholarships and decorums at third or fourth removes (he calls it culture), and built up from them. . . .[14]

* * *

The best part of Emersonianism is, it breeds the giant that destroys itself. Who wants to be any man's mere follower? lurks behind every page. No teacher ever taught, that has so provided for his pupil's setting up independently—no truer evolutionist.[15]

D.H. Lawrence [1885-1930]

Emerson believes in having the courage to treat all men as equals. It takes some courage *not* to treat them so now.

"Shall I not treat all men as gods?" he cries.

If you like, Waldo, but we've got to pay for it, when you've made them *feel* that they're gods. A hundred million American godlets is rather much for the world to deal with.

The fact of the matter is, all those gorgeous inrushes of exaltation and spiritual energy which made Emerson a great man, now make us sick. They are with us a drug habit. . . .

. . . I like Emerson's real courage. I like his wild and genuine belief in the Oversoul and the inrushes he got from it. But it is a museum-interest. Or else it is a taste of the old drug to the old spiritual drug-fiend in me.

We've got to have a different sort of sardonic courage.[16]

Robert Frost [1874-1963]

A young fellow came to me to complain of the department of philosophy in his university. There wasn't a philosopher in it. "I can't stand it." He was really complaining of his situation. He wasn't where he could feel real. But I didn't tell him so I didn't go into that. I agreed with him that there wasn't a philosopher in his university—there was hardly ever more than one at a time in the world—and I advised him to quit. . . .[17]

* * *

No subversive myself, I think it very Emersonian of me that I am so sympathetic with subversives, rebels, runners out, runners out ahead, eccentrics, and radicals.[18]

Eminent Estimations: An Encomium

1. *Memoirs of Margaret Fuller Ossoli.* W. H. Channing, J. F. Clarke, and R. W. Emerson, eds. Boston, 1852, vol. I, p. 194-195.
2. Fuller, Margaret. December 7, 1844. Reprinted in *The Recognition of Ralph Waldo Emerson.* M. R. Konvitz, ed. Ann Arbor: The University of Michigan Press, 1972, p. 24.
3. Norton, Andrews. August 27, 1838. *Ibid.,* 7.
4. James, Henry. From *Partial Portraits* (1888). Reprinted in *Literary Criticism.* L. Edel, ed. New York: The Library of America, 1984, p. 253.
5. *Ibid.,* 262.
6. James, William. "Address at the Emerson Centenary in Concord" (1903). From *Memories and Studies* (1911). Reprinted in *Emerson: A Collection of Critical Essays.* M. R. Konvitz and S. E. Whicher, eds. Englewood Cliffs, NJ: Prentice-Hall, 1962, p. 22.
7. Santayana, George. "Emerson." From *Interpretations of Poetry and Religion* (1900). *Ibid.,* 32.
8. Peabody, Elizabeth Palmer. "Nature—A Prose Poem." *United States Magazine, and Democratic Review* (February 1838). Reprinted in *Critical Essays on Ralph Waldo Emerson.* R. E. Burkholder and J. Myerson, eds. Boston: G. K. Hall, 1983, p. 28.
9. Nietzsche, Friedrich. *Twilight of the Idols: Or, How to Philosophize with the Hammer.* Richard Polt, tr. Indianapolis: Hackett Publishing Company, Inc., 1997, p. 58-9. The translator points out that the original saying from Ovid (*Epistulae Ex Ponto* III, 4, 79) has *voluntas* (will) rather than *voluptas* (lust).
10. Arnold, Matthew. *Discourses in America* (1885). Reprinted in Konvitz (1972), 68.
11. *Ibid.,* 70-73.
12. Dewey, John. "Ralph Waldo Emerson." *Characters and Events* (1929). Reprinted in Konvitz and Whicher (1962), 24.
13. Woolf, Virginia. A review of *Journals of Ralph Waldo Emerson,* 1820-32. *The Times Literary Supplement,* March 3, 1910. Reprinted in *Books and Portraits.* Mary Lyon, ed. New York: Harcourt Brace Jovanovich, 1977, p. 71.
14. Whitman, Walt. *Specimen Days and Collect* (1882-1883). Reprinted in Konvitz (1972), 64.
15. *Ibid.,* 65.
16. Lawrence, D.H. From a review of Stuart Sherman's *Americans,* printed in the *Dial* (1923). *Ibid.,* 168.
17. Frost, Robert. "On Emerson." Daedalus (Fall, 1959). Reprinted in Konvitz and Whicher (1962), 16.
18. *Ibid.*

Emerson in Conversation: A Bibliographical Conclusion

In this introduction to Emerson, I have aimed not to simplify Emerson's writings, but to commend this spectrum of performances by offering an incipient indication of their insight and intrigue. Introductory remarks serve us best when they avoid quick summary, hasty conclusion, and the installation of inhibiting locutions. An introduction should, instead, turn the reader to the *potential* of what is being introduced. One reads an introduction not to find answers, but to inquire after a beginning, or at least, some recommendations for continued investigations. I have, therefore, not worked to exhibit a comprehensive or complete Emerson, but to stimulate the sense that the words here offered have to be initial, superficial, and, at best, gestures toward wider and deeper possibilities of reading and research.

There are thousands of essays and books that bear reference to Emerson. One may glean some sense of this vast catalogue by soliciting extensive bibliographies (e.g., Myerson (1982 and 2000), or Porte (2001)), which orient the reader and researcher to the scope and grandeur of the prospective terrain. Using the bibliography as a compass signals how one's own mapping and mapmaking may commence or continue.

EMERSON'S WRITING (Selected)

The Complete Sermons of Ralph Waldo Emerson. 4 vols. A.J. von Frank, A.R. Toulouse, A. Delbanco, R. Bosco, and W.T. Mott, eds. Columbia: University of Missouri Press, 1989-1992.
The Complete Works of Ralph Waldo Emerson. Centenary Edition. 12

vols. E.W. Emerson, ed. Boston: Houghton Mifflin, 1903-04.
The Correspondence of Emerson and Carlyle. Joseph Slater, ed. New
York: Columbia University Press, 1964.
Emerson's Antislavery Writings. Len Gougeon and Joel Myerson, eds.
New Haven: Yale University Press, 1995.
The Journals and Miscellaneous Notebooks of Ralph Waldo Emerson.
16 vols. W.H. Gilman, A.R. Ferguson, G.P. Clark, et al., eds.
Cambridge, MA: Harvard University Press, 1960-1982.
The Letters of Ralph Waldo Emerson. 10 vols. R.L. Rusk and E.M.
Tilton, eds. New York: Columbia University Press, 1939-95.
Ralph Waldo Emerson: Essays and Lectures. Joel Porte, ed. New
York: Library of America, 1983.
Ralph Waldo Emerson: Collected Poems and Translations. Harold
Bloom and Paul Kane, eds. New York: Library of America, 1994.
ANTHOLOGIES
Emerson in His Journals. Joel Porte, ed. Cambridge, MA: Belknap
Press of Harvard University Press, 1982.
Emerson's Prose and Poetry. Joel Porte and Saundra Morris, eds.
New York: W.W. Norton & Company, 2001.
Selections from Ralph Waldo Emerson: An Organic Anthology.
Stephen E. Whicher, ed. Boston: Houghton Mifflin, 1957.
The Selected Writings of Ralph Waldo Emerson. Brooks Atkinson, ed.
New York: The Modern Library, 1992.
BIOGRAPHIES
Cabot, James Elliot. *A Memoir of Ralph Waldo Emerson.* 2 vols.
Boston: Houghton Mifflin, 1887.
McAleer, John. *Ralph Waldo Emerson: Days of Encounter.* Boston:
Little, Brown, 1984.
Richardson, Robert D. *Emerson: The Mind on Fire.* Berkeley:
University of California Press, 1995.
HISTORY
Garvey, T. Gregory, ed. *The Emerson Dilemma: Essays on Emerson
and Social Reform.* Athens: The U of Georgia P, 2001.
Howe, Daniel Walker. *The Unitarian Conscience: Harvard Moral
Philosophy, 1805-1861.* Cambridge, MA: Harvard UP, 1970.
BIBLIOGRAPHIES
Burkholder, R. E. and J. Myerson. *Emerson: An Annotated Secondary
Bibliography.* Pittsburgh: University of Pittsburgh Press, 1985.
Myerson, Joel. *Ralph Waldo Emerson: A Descriptive Bibliography.*
Pittsburgh: University of Pittsburgh Press, 1982.
Myerson, Joel, ed. *A Historical Guide to Ralph Waldo Emerson.* New
York: Oxford University Press, 2000.